# AUSTRALIAN
# WILDLIFE
## ON YOUR DOORSTEP

This second edition published in 2023 by Reed New Holland Publishers
First published in 2019 by Reed New Holland Publishers
Sydney

Level 1, 178 Fox Valley Road, Wahroonga, NSW 2076, Australia

newhollandpublishers.com

A record of this book is held at the National Library of Australia.

ISBN 978 1 92107 320 5

Managing Director: Fiona Schultz
Publisher and Project Editor: Simon Papps
Designers: Cyb Elizalde and Andrew Davies
Production Director: Arlene Gippert
Printed in China

10 9 8 7 6 5 4 3 2 1

Keep up with Reed New Holland
and New Holland Publishers
 ReedNewHolland
 @NewHollandPublishers and @ReedNewHolland

## ABOUT THE AUTHOR

For almost 25 years Stephanie Jackson's work as a
freelance travel writer and photographer has revolved
around her passion for wildlife and has taken her on
extensive journeys around Australia. Her images have
been published in newspapers, text books, magazines
and calendars, and have also used by Australian
tourism authorities in their promotional
material and on their websites.

# AUSTRALIAN
# WILDLIFE
## ON YOUR DOORSTEP

SECOND EDITION

STEPHANIE JACKSON

Australian Pelican at the beach beside a camping area at Woody Head, near Iluka, New South Wales.

# CONTENTS

Male King Parrot in the author's garden.

# INTRODUCTION

As an adventurous child I had an insatiable passion for wildlife, and I collected every dead creature that I discovered on my rambles through the countryside. Starfish that had been abandoned on the beach by the retreating tide, birds that lay, as though sleeping, in fields and woodlands, and insects that had come to the end of their brief lives were all carried home to my bedroom that was crammed with more active specimens. The spiders, beetles and snails that thrived in a cluster of dusty jars were my childhood companions, and when I unearthed worms and other wriggling creatures that lived within the damp soil of the garden I was as enthralled by these treasures as other people might have been by the discovery of gold or diamonds.

My mother, frustrated by the smell of rotting carcasses that emanated from my room and by my habit of arriving at the dinner table with dirt under my fingernails and a newly discovered beetle in my hand, finally put her foot down and attempted to channel my interests in other directions, but my passion for Mother Nature's astounding diversity of wild creatures remained undiminished.

For the last 40 years I've lived and worked on a rural property in south-eastern Queensland, and I share my secluded retreat, with its sprawling gardens that are hemmed with untamed bushland and eucalypt forests, with a community of mammals, birds, reptiles, frogs, insects and spiders. As I glimpse the intimate details of their lives, I'm continually enthralled by the diverse behaviours and unique personalities of my wild, yet welcome neighbours. It's here that I've photographed more than 65 per cent of the species featured in this book, and with the majority of the other wild creatures that are illustrated in the following pages having been encountered in rural and urban regions within a 50km radius of this wildlife haven, I can honestly boast that a staggering diversity of wildlife thrives on my doorstep.

Almost 90 per cent of Australians live in urban areas, and many explore the natural world only via television documentaries that offer visions of the wondrous creatures of Australia and of distant lands. Who can deny that they've been mesmerized by the antics of Alaskan bears, enthralled by the hunting prowess of the great cats of Africa, and awestruck by the elegance of an eagle's chick as it steps courageously from its cliff-top nest and takes its first flight on an unseen breeze? These are glimpses of wildlife that most people will never see at first hand, but amazing events are happening in Australia every day, and some of the most spectacular creatures on the planet are right on the doorstep of each and every one of us, if we take the time to explore our own backyard.

This vast continent has a greater diversity of wildlife than any other developed country, but sadly it has a less enviable claim to fame, for Australia has the worst rate of mammal extinction in the world. Eighteen species of mammals and many species of birds and frogs have become extinct in the last 200 years, and it's the actions of the human race that have played a major role in their demise.

Land clearing has destroyed and fragmented wildlife habitats. Huge populations of feral animals, including rabbits, pigs and camels that rampage across the landscape and damage fragile ecosystems, have also had a dramatic impact on wildlife communities. Several native species are being nudged towards oblivion by feral cats, silent and stealthy assassins that, with a population of up to 6.3 million, slaughter a million birds every day.

It's not all doom and gloom however, for although some species struggle to survive, others have adapted well to the changing environment and have set up home in suburbia. Possums doze in the dark corners of sheds; gulls and ibis feast at rubbish tips; lorikeets and bats roost in the trees of parklands and scoff the sweet fruits of backyard trees; reptiles sun themselves in quiet gardens; geckos and spiders secrete themselves in the dim corners of houses; and frogs make themselves at home in garden pools. There's no room for complacency, though, for the threats to Australia's unique wildlife have not abated.

The long-term survival of the human race is inexorably linked to the health of the natural environment and the great diversity of creatures, both large and small, with which we coexist on Planet Earth. The task of caring for the environment cannot be left entirely in the hands of governments and organisations dedicated to the cause. It is the responsibility of us all, and although it's often said that one person's actions have no significant impact on a situation of national or global importance, that's not always correct. Like a raindrop that unites with countless others to convert a tranquil stream to a raging river, even the smallest of actions can have an impact on the world around us, and everyone can play a valuable role in protecting the natural environment and ensuring the survival of the remarkable creatures that are right on the doorstep of each and every one of us.

## Species names

The species names of the animals used in the book adhere to those found in the following titles:

Anstis, M. 2017. *Tadpoles and Frogs of Australia.* Second Edition. Reed New Holland.

Framenau, V., Baehr, B., and Zborowski, P. 2014. *A Guide to the Spiders of Australia.* Reed New Holland.

Slater, P., Slater, P., and Slater, R. 2009. *The Slater Field Guide to Australian Birds.* Second Edition. Reed New Holland.

van Dyck, S., Gynther, I., and Baker, A. 2013. *Field Companion to the Mammals of Australia.* Reed New Holland.

Wilson, S. and Swann, G. 2021. *A Complete Guide to Reptiles of Australia.* Sixth Edition. Reed New Holland.

Zborowski, P. and Storey, R. 2017. *A Field Guide to Insects in Australia.* Fourth Edition. Reed New Holland.

Eastern Grey Kangaroo mother and joey.

# WILDLIFE HABITATS

## NATIONAL PARKS

**M**any of Australia's most important wildlife habitats are situated within national parks and other protected areas that cover almost 12 per cent of the continent. More than 680 national parks sprawl across mountain ranges, vast swathes of the outback, and immense deserts. They embrace long segments of the coastline, and incorporate wetlands of international significance, together with rainforests, rivers and lakes. The good news is that many parks are only a short distance from the nation's most populous cities, which means that for the 66 per cent of the population who live in a capital city, the staggering diversity of creatures that thrive in these wild neighbourhoods are almost on the doorstep.

The Lane Cove National Park, where creeks and rivers mutter seductively through eucalypt forests, is merely 16km from the throbbing heart of Sydney. In the Sydney Harbour National Park wildlife thrives in an environment that encompasses woodlands, rugged cliffs and secluded beaches. Only a short distance away from the chaotic centre of the city lie the forests and coastal landscapes of the Royal National Park, which is home to more than 300 species of birds.

It's the Dandenong Ranges National Park, which is less than 50km from the hurly-burly of Melbourne, which lures that city's residents to the great outdoors. In this 3,500-hectare park, forests dominated by the mighty Mountain Ash, one of the world's tallest tree species, are severed by gullies congested with tree ferns, wombats waddle through lush vegetation, lyrebirds scurry nervously from one shaded retreat to another and goannas hunt for food among the confusion of debris on the forest floor.

The Mount Lofty Ranges rise from the plains on which the South Australian city of Adelaide sits, and here, 13km from the hub of this attractive metropolis, lies the quiet world of Belair National Park where Southern Brown Bandicoots are the most conspicuous wild creatures.

And on the island state of Tasmania, Mount Field National Park, where wildlife thrives among a landscape dominated by waterfalls, rainforests and alpine moorlands, is on the doorstep of the residents of the city of Hobart.

Polblue Swamp (above) and
Blackdown Tablelands National Park (below).

In Western Australia, John Forrest National Park beckons the citizens of Perth to a wild refuge that's only 24km from the CBD, and in a landscape where waterfalls splash among dense forests, it's not hard to spot some of the park's 10 species of mammals, 91 species of birds and 23 species of reptiles.

For the residents of the Australian Capital Territory, the site of the national parliament, an escape from urban chaos is easy too, for the Namadgi National Park, which is home to 35 species of mammals, and where alpine meadows are crowned with mountain peaks and granite cliffs rise among snow gum woodlands, is merely 30km away from the cut and thrust of political life.

Further north, the spectacular D'Aguilar National Park is only a 10-minute drive from the centre of the Queensland capital of Brisbane. With hills cloaked with both eucalypt forests and rainforests that toss their shade over streams inhabited by Platypuses, this 36,000-hectare park is home to numerous species of birds and more than 200 species of animals.

Darwin, the capital of the Northern Territory, is more than 300km from any other major town, but Territorians are not intimated by the tyranny of distance, for every journey beyond the suburbs is a long one, and although the 250km drive to reach Kakadu National Park means that

The Flinders Ranges National Park, South Australia, is a hot-spot for wildlife.

it's certainly not on the city's doorstep, it's definitely in the backyard of those who live in this remote neck of the woods.

This spectacular wilderness area, which covers 20,000 square kilometres and is Australia's largest national park, has an astounding diversity of landscapes, from coastal areas with secluded bays, sandy beaches and mangrove swamps, to vast plains and wetlands hemmed with rocky escarpments from which waterfalls cascade into tranquil pools. There's an equally diverse range of wildlife here too, with around 10,000 crocodiles and some 280 bird species, including an estimated 3 million Magpie Geese, calling the park home.

There are no great cities in the Australia outback, but with many national parks located in the country's often-arid interior, wildlife is routinely on the doorstep not only of those who live and work in the region, but also of the hordes of tourists and grey nomads who make a pilgrimage to the outback every year. Despite the routinely harsh climatic conditions, vast mobs of kangaroos, huge flocks of emus, many species of birds and some unique reptiles thrive in the national parks that are within cooee of remote outback townships.

For much of the year the outback shows only its desolate face, but when rains arrive and waterholes and ephemeral lakes are filled to the brim, vast populations of migratory birds move in to stake their claim to prime outback habitats. Anyone who spends some time in the most remote of national parks or who wanders only a short distance from their urban home will discover that the wild side of this great country is never far away.

Dingoes often wander along the beaches of Queensland's Fraser Island.

# COASTAL REGIONS

**A**ustralians have a love affair with the coast that is part of the nation's vast outdoor playground, but every year millions of foreign visitors arrive on the continent's sunny shores, for the coast is the favoured habitat of some 2 million birds, of approximately 50 species, that migrate from the northern hemisphere to take advantage of the warmer climate.

There's a permanent population of some 1.1 million shorebirds of approximately 26 species, but there's ample room for the immense flocks of migratory birds however, for the coastline that hems the continent and its islands, many of which are the favoured breeding sites of shorebirds, covers a staggering 59,700km. Although 85 per cent of Australians live within 50km of the coast, it's still possible to find pristine and deserted beaches that are devoid of any hint of the existence of *Homo sapiens*.

Bustling cities, quiet towns and villages that appear almost comatose are clustered along the coastal fringe where ocean breezes bring a touch of relief on scorching summer days, but the natural environment and wildlife have both paid a hefty price for humanity's passion for coastal living. Homes with an ocean view, tourist resorts offering direct access to beaches, marinas crammed with the symbols of an affluent lifestyle, and

The coastal vegetation of Grassy Head, New South Wales, is inhabited by a wide range of wildlife.

Plenty of aquatic creatures can be found in the rock pools on Fraser Island, Queensland.

ports servicing global industries have come at a cost to wildlife, with their habitats destroyed or fragmented by the destruction of sand dunes, the draining of wetlands, the removal of mangrove forests and the clearing of coastal vegetation.

Many insects, reptiles and birds thrive among the vegetation of coastal dunes. Other species inhabit wetlands, forests and heaths, but it's mangroves, which rise from the nutrient-rich mud of river estuaries, that are home to the most diverse and vibrant communities of coastal wildlife. Their maze of supportive roots provides a sanctuary that's utilised by some 75 per cent of all marine animals at some stage of their lifecycle, and it's here that young fish, crustaceans and molluscs seek shelter from predators, and thrive and grow in calm and shallow waters. In the mangroves' branches, birds that require tidal roosts relax in the shade, content in the knowledge that the food that the ocean generously provides is right at their feet.

Despite the continuing loss of wildlife habitats, it's never hard to discover birds and animals on Australia's rocky coastal headlands and cliffs, among its verdant fringing forests, and on the more than 10,000 beaches that divide the land from the sea. Oystercatchers dabble among rocky pools; pelicans clamour for scraps tossed by anglers; battalions of blue soldier crabs march across the wet sand; hermit crabs parade in their newly acquired shell homes; turtles come ashore

Birds nest among the windswept vegetation of the Yorke Peninsula, South Australia.

to lay their eggs; and majestic Brahminy Kites snatch their unsuspecting prey from azure waters.

Anyone who's prepared to peer into the ocean will discover a staggering diversity of wildlife here too, and the Great Barrier Reef, a World Heritage listed area off the Queensland coast, is as good as it gets, for here dugongs and marine turtles, dolphins and whales, and more than 1,500 species of fish, inhabit the world's largest coral ecosystem that's right on Australia's doorstep.

Social progress, commercial development and employment opportunities are often cited as justification for the destruction of coastal environments, but Mother Nature refuses to sit idly by as the heavy hand of humans takes its toll on the landscape. She enlists her allies, the wind and the sea, that send waves, wiped up by storms, rushing in from the ocean to rip at the shore that, with its cloak of vegetation long gone, is left naked and defenceless. Mighty trees topple into the sea that, in its wildest moods, threatens to sweep away waterfront buildings constructed on fragile sand dunes, and raging waters roar into river estuaries, battering the coast that was once hemmed with forests and mangrove trees.

Human activities have left Mother Nature with many wounds to heal, but despite the detrimental impact that modern civilisation has had on the environment, many resilient creatures continue to thrive in the varied habitats that can still be found on the doorstep of every coastal settlement.

The forested banks of the Mann River, northern New South Wales, are the habitat of many species of wildlife.

# RIVERS, LAKES AND OTHER WETLANDS

Australia is a very dry continent but, despite that fact, it has substantial rivers, lakes and wetlands, all of which support diverse communities of wildlife.

The most important waterway is the Murray River that, together with the Darling River and other minor tributaries, forms the country's longest river system that makes its contorted 3,672km journey from south-western Queensland to its gaping estuary in South Australia.

Sprawling cities, bustling towns and sleepy villages lie on the banks of this and other river systems, and with parklands, native woodlands and residential areas lining many of these waterways, wildlife is never far from the doorstep of urban residents, for where there's permanent water, there's inevitably life.

Fairy-wrens and finches twitter and insects flutter among low reeds and grasses that hem rivers, lakes and wetlands and provide the smallest of wild creatures with safe havens from predators, from inclement weather and from the scorching rays of the summer sun. A confusion of riverbank shrubs with dense foliage offers shelter and nesting sites for larger birds, including honeyeaters that feast on the nectar produced by flowering plants that dabble their roots in the water. Parrots, owls and possums raise their families in hollows in the gnarled trunks of the eucalypt giants of riverine forests. Butterflies and dragonflies drift past on subtle breezes, and at the water's edge, wading birds probe the dark mud for their prey, frogs hide among damp vegetation, and lizards and turtles demonstrate that life was definitely meant to be easy as they lazily soak up the day's warmth on sunlit logs.

Humans, over the brief period of European settlement of this immense island continent, have changed the course of many rivers, stemmed their flows with weirs and dams that have created vast lakes where none, without human intervention, would

There's an abundance of wildlife in the hills surrounding Lake Glenbawn, which is on the doorstep of Scone, New South Wales.

Above and opposite: Dunn's Swamp in Wollemi National Park, New South Wales, is a birdwatcher's paradise.

ever have existed, sucked them dry for the irrigation of crops, and polluted them with chemicals and with agricultural and industrial runoff. Some species of wildlife have paid a heavy price for the deteriorating quality of the water and the dramatic changes that humanity has imposed on the landscape.

With river flows reduced or diverted, many of the country's major rivers, minor streams, lakes and wetlands have been deprived of water. Add the impact of droughts, which have increased in frequency and intensity in recent decades, and the clearing of wetland vegetation for agricultural and urban development to the mix and it's easy to comprehend why some

populations of wildlife have struggled to survive or been forced to find new habitats.

Many artificial lakes, including those that lie in the valleys of the Snowy Mountains of New South Wales, in the forested ranges of the Tasmanian wilderness, and in Western Australia, fought their way into existence in the face of vigorous public opposition. Although their creation came at great cost to the environment, with valleys permanently inundated and wildlife habitats obliterated, the passing years have brought new life and healed the scars of progress that once blighted the landscape.

The damming of the Ord River in the 1970s had a dramatic impact on the semi-arid Kimberley region of north-western

Australia, for the project gave birth to Lake Argyle, the largest artificial lake in the southern hemisphere. With its calm waters covering almost 1,000 square kilometres, it has gradually evolved to become a Ramsar protected wetland that's teeming with wildlife, including 270 species of birds and an estimated 35,000 Freshwater Crocodiles.

Such large bodies of water, extensive wetlands and mighty rivers are all of great importance for many communities of wildlife, but so too are the less imposing sources of water that are scattered across the continent. Streams that are often little more than a series of muddy waterholes, the shallow ephemeral salt lakes of arid inland regions, and secluded reed-choked swamps all provide vital natural habitats for countless species of wildlife.

In Australia, water frequently plays a role in recreational activities, with fishing and boating, together with camping and picnicking beside a picturesque waterway or lake, all being traditional components of the great Australian way of life. With water frequently on the doorstep of urban areas and holiday destinations, a close encounter with some of the many species of wildlife that call the aquatic world their home is almost guaranteed.

Wildflowers, which bloom in the outback after rain, attract both insects and birds.

# OUTBACK REGIONS

The outback is often regarded as a region that's dominated by deserts, that's barren, arid and inhospitable, and that's home only to reptiles and a few other hardy creatures, but that's far from the truth, for there's more to see here than swathes of sand and barren stony plains that stretch to every distant horizon. There's an abundance of wild creatures that are well adapted for survival in the harsh climatic conditions, and that rely on plants that are tough and determined survivors too.

Spinifex grass is the dominant species of vegetation in many inland areas, and large clumps of this viciously spiny plant offer an inviting habitat for small mammals, reptiles and ground-dwelling birds that require not only shelter but also protection from predators. Carpets of saltbush provide wildlife with food and a place to call home. Mitchell grass, which cloaks vast outback plains, supports huge mobs of grazing kangaroos that utilise woodlands dominated by acacia and eucalyptus trees as shady retreats. The tangled vegetation that lines the banks of waterholes and meandering rivers and streams provides food and shelter for a menagerie of small creatures that call the outback home.

Sadly, the outback includes many far from pristine environments, for even here, in some of the continent's most remote locations, the delicate balance of nature has been dramatically altered by human activities. Permanent supplies of water in stock troughs and dams have allowed vast mobs of kangaroos and huge flocks of emus and other birds to thrive in areas where their populations would once have been reduced as the weakest succumbed to thirst during periods of intense drought.

The increased availability of water has also benefited feral animals, which have had a significant impact on the fragile ecosystems of the outback. Rabbits devour vegetation that, in pre-European times, would have provided sustenance for native animals. Feral cats and foxes are implicated in the demise of many communities of small birds and animals, and wild camels, with their population estimated to be in excess of 1 million, roam across central Australia where they foul waterholes that are utilised by native wildlife, and feed on more than 80 per cent of all plant species.

During times of drought the outback grimaces with the face of despair and death, but it's also a time of plenty when birds of prey and other carnivores, such as dingoes, pick the landscape and its sun-bleached corpses clean. When rains eventually fall, and when water fills every dry riverbed and lake and spills out over extensive floodplains, Mother Nature calls for wildlife to return, and new life blossoms

Outback waterholes attract large numbers of birds and animals.

The drought-tolerant plants of the outback provide safe havens for many small creatures.

with a profusion of wildflowers that attract insects and nectar-feeding birds. Every now and then, when the great expanse of glinting white salt that is Lake Eyre is transformed into a spectacular inland sea that covers some 9,690 square kilometres, 6–8 million water birds of around 60 species make the pilgrimage to the South Australian outback to gorge themselves on an abundance of food, to breed and to raise their young.

For the residents of the towns of the outback, wildlife is never far away, in fact, in some small settlements it's not uncommon for kangaroos to graze on urban lawns, for emus to wander along the main street, and for Koalas to doze in eucalyptus trees that toss their welcome shade over dusty homes. Travellers who are in the right place at the right time can enjoy the enviable experience of having an abundance of wild creatures on the doorstep as they soak up the wonders of the outback from a campsite beside a desert waterhole, among shady woodlands, beside a tranquil stream or on the shores of an azure lake.

At Mount Chambers Gorge, northern South Australia, wildlife was on the doorstep of the author's campervan.

The Snowy River originates at Mount Kosciuszko, New South Wales, and flows south to reach the ocean in eastern Victoria.

# ALPINE REGIONS

**W**hen it comes to alpine regions Australia is not in the same league as continents where great mountain ranges spear into the skies, for the country's highest peak, Mount Kosciuszko, which rises to a height of merely 2,228m, is tiny in comparison to the world's greatest mountains.

The continent's only truly alpine region is in the Australian Alps, a mountain range that covers almost 233,000 hectares, and that straddles eastern Victoria, south-eastern New South Wales, and the Australian Capital Territory. It's part of the Great Dividing Range, the 3,000km-long jagged spine that divides the eastern coast of Australia from the lowlands of the interior, and that consists of the Snowy Mountains, the Brindabella Range and the more southerly Victorian Alps.

Much of this alpine region lies within the Kosciuszko National Park in New South Wales and Victoria's Alpine National Park, and it's the protection that this status has offered, in addition to the region's harsh winter climate and rugged terrain, that have ensured much of the landscape and its amazing diversity of flora and fauna has remained untouched by the punishing hand of human activities.

Although there are several towns in the valleys below the foothills of the Australian

The Alpine Way traverses the Snowy Mountains in New South Wales.

Mount Samaria, Victoria, is a haven for wildlife.

The Snowy Mountains (above) and Mount Samaria (opposite) provide habitats for a wide range of species.

Alps, there are few permanent settlements in the highest regions, other than ski resorts and the New South Wales town of Cabramurra, which is the highest permanently inhabited town in the country. With minimal development, the biodiversity of the alpine region remains in relatively good health, and more than 40 species of mammals, 200 species of birds, 30 species of reptiles, and 15 species of amphibians continue their lives here as they have done for millennia.

At the first hint of winter's approach, many birds and animals retreat to lower areas of the ranges and others migrate to warmer regions, but some have no need to leave, for they know exactly how to cope when the icy hand of winter strikes their world.

The Dusky Antechinus, a tiny marsupial, survives by living under the snow, while other diminutive creatures, such as the Mountain Pygmy-possum, settle down to hibernate throughout the winter months.

With the climate of the highest areas of the alpine region being too cold for all but a few hardy avian residents, the majority of birds opt for the easy life and inhabit the grasslands and forests of lower areas where the weather is more amenable and where food is more abundant.

Reptiles, which are among the most resilient and versatile members of the region's wildlife community, can be found throughout the mountainous terrain, even on the highest peaks. When winter hints that its return is imminent, some migrate to lower and warmer regions, while others seek out a secluded haven that will provide them with adequate protection from the worst of the winter's icy weather. They slither into deep and narrow rocky crevices, and venture outside only occasionally to catch a snack of the insects that, as their major source of food, allow reptiles to survive in a hostile environment.

When spring inevitably returns and temperatures rise, wildflowers blossom and the wild creatures of the Australian Alps return, and although their varied habitats might be right on the doorstep of holiday accommodation and popular camping areas, many of the wild residents of the mountains are far from easy to see.

Wombats quietly emerge from their cavernous burrows and possums scamper among the branches of trees only under the cover of darkness. Koalas sit motionlessly in lofty eucalyptus trees, their thick silvery grey fur ensuring that they're well camouflaged on the trunks of the trees that provide them with the leaves that are their only food. Flying-foxes are well hidden too as they spend their days dozing in the trees, but kangaroos and wallabies are more conspicuous as they bound across grasslands and rush through woodland vegetation before disappearing from sight in little more than the blink of an eye.

Even on a misty winter's morning there are plenty of birds in the Blue Mountains Botanic Gardens, New South Wales.

# URBAN PARKS

As far back as 1810 Australian town planners recognised the need to establish public parks in urban areas. It was then that Lachlan Macquarie, the governor of the fledgling colony, dedicated an area for "the recreation and amusement of the inhabitants of the town," and Sydney's first public park was born.

Hyde Park has evolved into a welcoming retreat for more than merely the city's human population however, for Common Brushtail Possums, rowdy colonies of flying-foxes, owls and ibis have all set up home in a wooded landscape that's within sight of hotels, department stores and streets bustling with traffic. The park provides a hint of wild Australia in the heart of urban chaos, and there are similar colonies of wildlife in parks that have been incorporated into the urban landscape in almost every city and town in Australia.

The survival of wildlife was probably of little, if any interest to early town planners who regarded public parks as nothing more than recreational precincts for the burgeoning human populations of urban areas. They were, and continue to be, environments that offer an escape from the noise, the congestion and the pollution of cities and towns, and they're idyllic locations for children to play, for lovers to meet in secret assignations and for families to stroll or enjoy a picnic in a healthy and tranquil environment.

If a park's designers have selected the most appropriate species of trees and other

There's plenty of wildlife around the Torrens River in Adelaide, in the heart of the capital of South Australia.

In Queensland, the lake in Tondoon Botanic Gardens, Gladstone, is home to large numbers of turtles and attracts many species of birds.

plants and have incorporated a permanent source of water into the landscape, birds, with the lure of food that the plants provide, will be happy to take up residence or to drop in for a snack on their way to somewhere else. In sprawling parklands and botanic gardens, where there are large stands of trees and extensive areas of water, aquatic birds will make themselves at home too, and may even raise their families right on the doorstep of suburbia.

A close encounter with some of the most beautiful creatures of wild Australia can be on the agenda of every visitor to an urban park or garden where nature routinely puts on an entertaining display with a diverse cast of performers. Parrots flutter and squawk as they feed on the seasonal flowers and seeds of trees and shrubs. Honeyeaters, with acrobatic antics, silently sip at the nectar of delicate blooms. Fairy-wrens and scrubwrens twitter among grasses and dense vegetation, flycatchers dance as they snatch a feast of insects from the air, and waterbirds parade across verdant lawns and drift lazily on the calm waters of ornamental lakes. Birds are not the only entertainers that grace the stage of urban parks.

Insects, which proliferate when flowers bloom, crawl, hop and slither among petals and foliage, and provide food for lizards and other reptiles that sun themselves on pathways and on the boulders of rockeries.

No matter how well designed they

The parklands that border the Torrens River are home to many species of birds and are right in the centre of Adelaide.

may be, urban parklands rarely replicate every detail of the varied natural habitats in which birds and animals thrive in the wild, but many creatures enthusiastically adapt to life in an artificial environment. With their fears diminished by years of living in close proximity to people, they eagerly accept any food that's offered, but humankind's generosity often comes with adverse consequences for wildlife. A readily available supply of food can encourage them to develop an increasing dependence on the sustenance provided by their well-intentioned benefactors, and can encourage them to breed in far greater numbers than their new environment can support. This, in turn, can lead to conflicts among the birds and animals themselves as their artificial habitats become excessively congested. With high levels of noise, with huge numbers of birds defecating on cars and buildings in the vicinity of an urban park, and with excessive populations of wildlife spilling out to feed in nearby home gardens and agricultural areas, the unbalanced state of nature can guarantee that some people are far from happy when wildlife arrives on their doorstep.

This water feature in the author's garden is visited by many species of birds.

# HOME GARDENS

Every home garden can become a habitat for wildlife, but if it's a bland environment with little more than a carpet of manicured lawn it will attract few creatures other than insects that are blown in on the wind, and a magpie that might be the early bird that gets the worm as it passes by on its way from one more alluring garden to another. Don't despair though, for it's easy, even in the smallest of outdoor spaces, to create a unique ecosystem that birds and other wild creatures will find irresistible.

The simple option of providing artificial food, such as bowls of seed and platters of bread and honey, will bring results almost overnight, but such practices can have detrimental effects on the long-term health of wildlife and lead to a dependence on a welfare system, which may result in problems when a free handout is no longer available to hungry birds and animals.

A balanced garden ecosystem with natural sources of food, permanent water and a variety of vegetation will encourage wildlife to drop by occasionally or to set up home in the garden on a permanent basis. The creation of such an environment begins with the establishment of plants that will attract insects.

Insects, which are a major source of food for many species of birds, frogs, reptiles and spiders, will enthusiastically feed on the nectar produced by the flowers of a wide range of herbs, and by the gaudy flowers of many species of annual plants.

With a wide range of flowering trees and

Dense vegetation provides a welcome retreat for birds.

shrubs, such as grevilleas and callistemons that will produce flowers with copious amounts of nectar, melaleucas that will also provide the bark that many birds use in the construction of their nests, and other plants with dense foliage that will offer small birds shelter and a safe haven from predators, the garden will eventually be buzzing with activity. When a selection of other plants are established, including grasses and acacias that produce an abundance of seeds, shrubs that provide succulent berries, and taller species that offer shade and roosting areas for birds, wildlife will inevitably drop by.

Among the first birds to arrive will be honeyeaters that will not only appreciate the garden's flowers, but will also feed on the insects that have been attracted to the welcoming environment. Spiders will inevitably arrive too, and these amazing creatures play a vital role as fearless warriors in the ongoing battle against insect pests. Many of the species on which spiders enthusiastically dine, such as grasshoppers and sap-sucking beetles, should be viewed as an integral part of the wild community of a balanced ecosystem, rather than the enemy, for they provide nutrient-rich food for many other creatures.

If there's no water available, birds will be little more than itinerant visitors, but with a water feature, which can range from a simple and inexpensive bird bath to a large and complex pond, our feathered friends will claim the area as their own domain. They won't be too impressed if a bird bath is merely plonked in the centre of an extensive lawn however, for on summer days the shallow water will become too hot to drink, and when they've quenched their thirst or washed their feathers, the birds will be hoping to settle down among the foliage of a nearby shrub or tree where they can relax in the shade and preen their feathers.

A water feature that has a thriving community of aquatic plants will also attract frogs which play a vital role in maintaining the health of any garden, primarily by feasting on insects. If logs and rocks are included in the garden landscape, lizards and other reptiles might take up residence in these cosy retreats and play their own unique role in maintaining a balanced environment.

Nesting boxes or hollow logs attached to the trunks of tall trees will persuade some species of birds to raise their families there, while possums, gliders, insect-eating micro bats and other nocturnal creatures will appreciate the shelter and protection from the elements and from predators that such artificial retreats offer.

Some not so welcome creatures, such as brush-turkeys, might occasionally appear on the scene, but in a well designed garden the good, the bad and the ugly will thrive and go about their daily lives in a harmonious ecosystem that can be created right on the doorstep of every home.

Permanent water and flowers attract a great range of wildlife.

Brahminy Kite over the ocean waves at Iluka, New South Wales.

# BIRDS

Australia is a birdwatcher's paradise, for more than 830 species call this great country home, and although some are migrants that come and go with the changing seasons, an estimated 600 species, the majority of which are found nowhere else on Earth, make Australia a permanent home and flutter or stroll across the nation's varied landscapes.

Some face continual threats from natural predators and from introduced species such as feral cats and foxes, but it's the activities of the human race that pose the most serious risk to the survival of many bird species.

Australia's ever-increasing human population continually demands additional land for agriculture, for industry and for urban development but it's not simply trees, shrubs and grasslands that are obliterated by the onslaught of grumbling machinery. It's the habitats of birds and other wild creatures that are irrevocably destroyed. Recent research has revealed that since Europeans first set foot on Australian soil some 250 years ago more than half of the 262 species of birds that call south-eastern Australia their home have each lost more than 60 per cent of their natural habitat.

Although the consequences of European settlement have been less severe in more northern regions of the continent, the survival of the birds that inhabit these regions is still threatened by human activities. It's estimated that in south-eastern and northern Queensland, where vast swathes of land are still being cleared, every hectare of forest that is destroyed has a negative impact on up to 180 different species of birds.

Rainbow Lorikeet feeding on the flowers of a corkwood tree in the author's garden.

Rainbow Lorikeet is surely Australia's most colourful bird.

# PARROTS

## RAINBOW LORIKEET
*Trichoglossus haematodus*

Australia has its share of famous characters, but in 1771 it was a Rainbow Lorikeet that earned a place in history when it became the first of Australia's 56 species of parrots to spread its wings over British shores. The bird's epic adventure had begun the previous year when it was captured in Botany Bay and became the pet of a Polynesian man named Tupaia who shared James Cook's voyage on board the *Endeavour*. Sadly, Tupaia died on the return journey to England, but the bird survived and was destined for immortality.

In 1774, Peter Brown, an illustrator who was later appointed as the Botanical Painter to the Prince of Wales, was awestruck by the bird's beauty, and included a portrait of the avian celebrity in his book *New Illustrations of Zoology*. This guaranteed the Rainbow Lorikeet another claim to fame as the first Australian parrot to be introduced to the world in a coloured illustration within a commercial publication.

Only someone with the vision of a fossilised amoeba could fail to be dazzled by a glimpse of a Rainbow Lorikeet, for its plumage includes all the hues of the brightest of rainbows, with both males and females having a blue head and neck, a vivid orange-red breast, a blue lower body, emerald-green wings, a red bill and piercing red eyes.

They inhabit woodlands and forests in eastern Australia, from Queensland's

These birds are familiar in parks and gardens.

tropical Cape York to southern Victoria and northern Tasmania, and thrive in coastal areas as far west as the Yorke Peninsula in South Australia. A 2021 survey showed that the Rainbow Lorikeet was the most commonly seen bird in Australia, but not everyone lays out the welcome mat. They're not native to Western Australia, but today an estimated 40,000 thrive in the greater Perth area – the descendants of captive birds released in the 1960s. With their population continuing to increase, these unwelcome interlopers, which cause extensive damage to fruit crops and compete with indigenous parrots for limited nesting sites, are a declared pest species in southern areas of the state.

With their raucous chattering and argumentative screeching these gregarious birds, which are often seen in the company of Scaly-breasted Lorikeets, are impossible to ignore. Two or three birds, particularly when disputing ownership of a feeding area, can sound like a rampaging crowd, and when immense numbers flutter among the foliage of trees to sip on nectar-laden flowers, any concept of the bush as a place of peace and quiet is immediately obliterated.

Inspecting a nesting hollow in a gum tree at Tannum Sands, Queensland.

Feeding on a fallen mango at Rosedale, Queensland.

Rainbow Lorikeets, which have a brush-like tip to their tongue to enable them to feed efficiently on nectar, dine on the flowers of a wide range of native trees and shrubs, including eucalypts, grevilleas, banksias and melaleucas, in addition to many introduced plant species. With amazing agility and acrobatic antics they clamber from flower to flower, often hanging upside-down to reach blooms on fragile stems, and erupt into a screeching frenzy when the need to defend their territory from other birds arises. When flowers are scarce they'll eat seeds and insects, but their craving for the sweet treats of life lures them to orchards and gardens where a single bird pecking at soft fruit, such as mangoes, papaws and grapes, is of little concern, but it's a different story when a large flock arrives for a feast. The result can be disastrous, and the battle to protect crops from hordes of Rainbow Lorikeets remains an ongoing dilemma for orchardists.

They're commonly seen in urban parks and in the heart of cities and towns where flowering trees hem congested roadways, and are often attracted to home gardens with the offer of bread and honey. This provides an opportunity for a close encounter with these beautiful birds, but neither bread nor honey include the essential nutrients that the birds require, and such a diet may be harmful to their long-term health. The better option to encourage nectar-feeding birds to a garden is to plant trees and shrubs that will not only provide them with a natural and healthy source of food, but will also create a welcoming habitat for other native species.

Rainbow Lorikeets, like the majority of Australian parrots, require hollows in old trees for nesting sites, and if these, together with ample sources of food and water are available, these glorious birds will survive and bring pleasure to the human race until the end of time.

# BUDGERIGAR

*Melopsittacus undulatus*

Budgerigars are the most popular pets in the world, after dogs and cats, and anyone who is unfamiliar with the humble budgie must be as rare as an elephant in a rhubarb tree.

They are attractive and amiable little birds, but one of the characteristics that have made them so popular is their ability to mimic the human voice. Many will mutter "Who's a pretty boy?" and other simple phrases, but a budgie named Puck had a lot more to say, and according to the 1995 *Guinness Book of World Records*, this tiny chatterbox was an avian master of the English language, with a vocabulary of 1,728 words.

Flocks of budgies fluttered across the Australian landscape long before modern humans strode onto the scene, but it was George Shaw, an English zoologist, who officially described the Budgerigar in 1805. In 1840, the renowned naturalist and illustrator John Gould brought live budgies to Britain when he returned from a voyage to Australia, and within a decade a captive-breeding scheme had begun.

The name 'Budgerigar' is thought to be a derivation of the Aboriginal word '*betche-gara*', which refers to something that's good to eat, and although indigenous Australians

Budgies drinking at an outback waterhole.

Above and opposite: Budgerigars around a camping area. These images were taken near Boulia, outback Queensland.

might have regarded the bird as tasty bush tucker, Europeans saw it in a different light. They christened it with the scientific name *Melopsittacus undulatus*, which hinted that the budgie had more than culinary appeal, for the first part of its name comes from a Greek word meaning 'melodious parrot', while the second part is a Latin word that translates as 'like waves', a reference to the ornate pattern on the bird's wings and the back of its head.

Budgies bred in captivity have plumage in a wide range of colours, from white and yellow, to green, mauve and blue, but their wild relatives are invariably green with bright yellow faces. There's little visible difference between males and females, other than the colour of the cere, the area surrounding the bird's nostrils, which is blue in males, brown or white in females and pink when the birds are immature.

Budgerigars are among the most numerous of all Australian parrots, with an estimated 5 million thriving in the wild. They're usually seen in relatively small flocks, but in good seasons, when there's an abundance of food, it's not uncommon to see hundreds of birds wheeling through the skies, twisting and turning in perfectly synchronised flight, or fluttering unexpectedly from trees like a deluge of falling leaves tossed into the air by the invisible hand of the wind.

They're most at home in semi-arid and arid inland areas of mainland Australia where they congregate in woodlands and grasslands, and although they inhabit much of the continent, they're not found in the far south-west, in the northern part of the Northern Territory or on the eastern coast.

The main component of the Budgerigar's diet is seeds of drought-tolerant grasses such as spinifex and Mitchell grass, and of herbaceous plants such as saltbush that carpet vast areas of the outback. They also dine on succulent foliage and on any fruit that may be available, and will gorge themselves on ripening crops of grain.

Budgies are nomadic, with their survival during droughts reliant on their instinct to migrate to areas where food and water are more readily available. They never travel far from a source of water however, and it's believed that Aboriginal people and early European settlers followed flocks of budgies and utilised their ability to locate water as part of their own survival strategies in an often arid environment.

Budgerigars are monogamous, and remain faithful to their one and only mate, and when it's time to start a family, the female lays her eggs in a hollow in a tree, or

occasionally in a log on the ground.

Subtle twittering emanating from shading foliage is a clue that budgies are taking it easy, but the best time to see these endearing little birds is at dawn when they flutter down from the skies to the edge of a tranquil waterhole or stream to quench their thirst before, with joyful twittering, heading off to enjoy their first snack of the day.

# LITTLE CORELLA
*Cacatua sanguinea*

There's a clue to the Little Corella's appearance hidden in its scientific name, for *sanguinea* is a reference to the blood-stained appearance of the feathers between the bird's eyes and its bill. This, together with the blue-grey patch of skin around each eye, provides a subtle contrast to the white plumage of the bird's head, its body and its wings. When in flight, the pale yellow plumage lining the underside of the bird's wings and broad tail is revealed.

The Little Corella, which inhabits semi-arid and arid regions across much of mainland Australia, is a species that elicits either love or hate. Watch it gently cooing with its life-long mate, quietly sipping on the nectar of the golden blooms of a silky oak tree, clambering among clusters of eucalyptus flowers, or nibbling on the seeds of grasses and legumes, and it's hard not to admire this attractive cockatoo. There's a flip side to its life however, and it's one that's not particularly appealing.

Little Corellas frequently congregate in flocks of hundreds of birds, and they're a raucous and argumentative mob as they flutter among the foliage of large trees, and squabble over roosting sites as they settle down for the night, and their chattering and screeching doesn't endear them to anyone

Feeding on flowers of a silky oak tree in parklands in Gympie, Queensland.

who finds these rowdy cockatoos taking up residence on their doorstep. During severe droughts, when immense flocks invade urban areas, it's not only their noise that makes them unwelcome. Thousands of birds defecate on pathways, buildings, and parked cars, and when they're in a destructive mood, they chew the stems and leaves of trees and reduce the foliage to tatters, with some trees eventually dying as a result of the persistent behaviour of these urban terrorists.

The darkness of the night brings a welcome silence, but disputes among Little Corellas resume at dawn, and when they finally head off to find a source of food, the screeching commotion continues as they launch themselves into the air from their lofty perches. Like fragile snowflakes at the mercy of a gale, they take to the skies in a blizzard of white plumage and vocal mayhem to feast, if other food is unavailable, on crops of ripening grain. Their insatiable appetite for cultivated crops ensures that they're far from popular with farmers.

As the breeding season approaches, each pair selects a hollow, usually in a eucalyptus tree that's close to water, where the female will eventually lay her eggs. There's plenty of aggression on display as birds defend their nesting site from others that come too close or threaten to hijack the cosy retreat that a pair may have used for several years. Eventually, with all disputes concluded and their ownership no longer under threat,

birds affectionately preen their mates with little sound other than subdued chattering, and it's then that Little Corellas, with their Jekyll and Hyde personalities, are among the most admired of all Australian parrots.

Little Corella at a camping area near Innamincka, outback South Australia.

Little Corellas in parklands in Maryborough, Queensland.

# LONG-BILLED CORELLA

*Cacatua tenuirostris*

An extended bill is not the only distinctive feature of the Long-billed

Feeding on spilt grain at railway yards near Sydney, New South Wales.

Corella, for with a dash of red plumage on its forehead and between its eyes and its bill, a similarly coloured collar across the top of its breast, blue-grey eye patches and predominantly white plumage, it's not hard to recognise this attractive bird that, when in flight, reveals yellow plumage beneath its wings.

Long-billed Corellas are found only in the south-eastern corner of the continent, in an area stretching from south-eastern South Australia and western Victoria to southern New South Wales, but other populations, which are believed to have been established as a result of the release of cagebirds, exist in some other parts of eastern Australia and in Western Australia.

These gregarious birds are often seen foraging on the ground, where they use their long bills to probe the soil for succulent insects and edible roots, and to pry fragments of bark from trees to reveal arboreal insects, but it's seeds that form a major part of the birds' diet. While the majority of the flock are feasting, a small number of their mates remain on sentry duty in nearby trees from where they give a raucous warning screech the moment any threat appears on the horizon. As far as farmers are concerned, it's the birds themselves, with their insatiable appetite for grain and sunflower seeds, which pose a very real threat.

The size of flocks is dependant on the availability of food, water and nesting sites, and in areas where these requirements are met, Long-billed Corellas have made themselves very unpopular, not only with farmers but also with urban residents, particularly those in wheat growing regions in Western Australia.

In recent years, when flocks of up to 10,000 birds invaded both towns and farmlands, the noise they caused, together with their faeces that were routinely plastered on cars, buildings, and footpaths, was more than most people could tolerate, and authorities were forced to consider culling the invading hordes. In their hunger for grain, the birds destroyed tarpaulins covering huge mounds of wheat at grain receival depots and gorged themselves on the treasure they unveiled. They stripped every skerrick of vegetation from riverbank gum trees, and commandeered every tree-trunk hollow for their nesting sites, leaving none vacant for other birds.

These attractive cockatoos form monogamous pairs, and when nesting hollows are unavailable, they'll look for alternative accommodation that might be merely a hole in the face of a stony cliff. While populations of Long-billed Corellas are declining in some parts of their range, their numbers have soared in Western Australia, thus ensuring that the species will thrive, to be admired or despised, for many centuries to come.

Long-billed Corellas in parklands in Maryborough, Queensland.

# KING PARROT

*Alisterus scapularis*

It was 1818 when German zoologist Martin Lichtenstein became the first to describe one of Australia's most beautiful native residents, and he was probably speechless with wonder as he gazed at the vividly coloured bird, for few wild creatures are more spectacular than His Highness the King Parrot.

With his brilliant red breast, head and underparts, emerald-green wings, long dark green tail, red bill and piercing dark eyes surrounded by a golden-yellow ring, the regal male dramatically overshadows his queen whose plumage is predominantly green, with only her lower belly being red.

Male King Parrot. All images taken in the author's garden.

Despite their gaudy plumage, King Parrots are surprisingly well camouflaged among the foliage of the woodlands and forests that are their primary habitat. The first hint of their presence may be a high-pitched squeak, or a flash of gaudy plumage as a bird flies past, momentarily adding a dash of brilliance to the shadows of the trees among which they forage for fruit, nuts, nectar, flowers and leaf buds, and dine on the seeds of acacias that are high on their list of favoured foods.

King Parrots, which live in pairs or small family groups, are found throughout eastern Australia, from northern Queensland to southern Victoria. They utilise hollows in old trees, primarily eucalypts, as nesting sites, but we humans have little hope of being able to take an inquisitive peek at the nest, at the bird's eggs, or at any developing chicks. The entrance to the hollow is usually several metres above the ground, but the parrot's nest is right at the bottom of the cavity, and thus well hidden not only from prying eyes, but also from predators, such as feral cats and reptiles.

These are inquisitive and confident birds that frequently visit urban parks and gardens if the food they require is available, as well as large trees in which to roost. They enthusiastically hop across manicured lawns, scoff fallen seeds and fruit, and tuck into tomatoes that are unprotected. It's not uncommon to see one of these dazzling birds peering down at the world from a gutter, a clothes line, or a power cable on the doorstep of some human habitation, but some birds might not look too happy.

Many King Parrots in the South Coast region of New South Wales have become the victims of Spironucleosis, a highly contagious, fast-spreading and often fatal disease. Infected birds quickly become emaciated and weak and as they lose the strength to fly they stagger about on the ground in a desperately miserable state.

Birds that congregate around garden bird baths or feeding tables are most at risk of being infected and spreading the disease to others. Anyone in this region who, with good intentions, routinely provides food and water to wild birds, can play a role in minimising the spread by ensuring that birds have access to nothing other than natural sources of food. Planting native trees and shrubs, particularly wattles and eucalypts, and allowing a lawn or other area of grass to grow a little taller than usual and thus produce seeds will give visiting birds the opportunity to forage for natural foods rather than encourage them to push and shove among hordes at a feeding table. While it might seem kind to provide birds with water to quench their thirst, it's best, in areas where Spironucleosis is rampant, to leave them to find their own water too – something they'll always be able to do except during the most severe of droughts.

Male eating a tomato.

Adult male and immature male at a bird bath.

Feeding on berries at Rushworth, Victoria.

Crimson Rosella feeding in parklands at Queen Mary Falls near Warwick, Queensland.

# CRIMSON ROSELLA

*Platycercus elegans*

The Crimson Rosella was first described in 1781 by John Latham who named it the Beautiful Lory, and there can be no disputing the fact that it's worthy of its original common name, for this is undoubtedly one of Australia's most spectacular parrots.

Australia is home to six species of rosellas, which are parrots within the genus *Platycercus*, and a distinctive feature of all six is their cheek-patches, with those of the Crimson Rosella being bright blue – a dramatic contrast to the vivid red plumage of the bird's head, its back and its breast. The gaudy adult Crimson Rosella certainly stands out from the crowd and is instantly recognisable, but immatures, with their predominantly olive-green plumage, are far less conspicuous in their camouflage dress.

They thrive in the forests and woodlands of eastern Australia, from south-eastern Queensland to south-eastern South Australia and Tasmania. Fruit, nectar, insects and seeds, particularly those of eucalyptus and acacia trees, feature prominently in the diet of Crimson Rosellas that dine both in the forest canopy and on the ground, but when they get their claws on the succulent fruit of commercial orchards, farmers are far from impressed, although few people complain when these attractive birds make themselves at home in urban parks and gardens.

They're monogamous birds that, during the breeding season, forage for food only with their mate. When they eventually decide to set up home together, they'll occasionally nest in a hole in an earthen embankment, but they usually opt for a tree-trunk hollow with an entrance high above the ground. They line the base of the hollow, which is generally well below the entrance, with scraps of wood and bark, aggressively defend their territory from intruders, and vigorously attack other birds that attempt to nest nearby.

Crimson Rosella at a nesting site near Hill End, New South Wales.

Although they're usually seen only in pairs or small groups, there's change in the air at the conclusion of the breeding season when juvenile Crimson Rosellas congregate in large flocks and chatter noisily as they forage together on the ground.

When in the treetops, these eye-catching parrots communicate with a wide range of sounds, from subtle bell-like calls to raucous screeching, but anyone who sees one of these glorious birds is sure to respond with little more than the silence of awestruck wonder.

# EASTERN ROSELLA
*Platycercus eximius*

When early European settlers discovered a spectacular multi-coloured parrot at Rose Hill, New South Wales, they named it the 'Rose Hill Parakeet'. The name evolved to become the 'Rosehiller' and finally the name 'Rosella' became the accepted term for the group of six Australian parrots, including the Eastern Rosella, which are included in the genus *Platycercus*.

Ask anyone to identify the colourful bird that's portrayed on packets of Arnott's biscuits and most will insist that it's an Eastern Rosella, but that's a long-held misconception. The company's prominent logo, which has been in use for more than 100 years, was created from a painting of a Mexican parrot that was given to the company's founder, William Arnott, by the captain of a coal-carrying ship that docked at the New South Wales port of Newcastle.

The Eastern Rosella's true claim to fame comes from its association with another long-established Australian company. Its image was adopted as the trademark of the Rosella Preserving and Manufacturing Company, and since 1895 this beautiful bird's portrait has graced bottles of Rosella tomato sauce to become an iconic part of the nation's culinary history.

The Eastern Rosella is found from Queensland to Victoria, in south-eastern

Eastern Rosellas bathing in a puddle near Scone, New South Wales.

Eastern Rosella at a caravan park at Repton, New South Wales.

South Australia, and in Tasmania where it not only inhabits open woodlands and grasslands that have adequate trees for roosting, but is also a common and welcome visitor to urban parklands and home gardens.

There are few birds that can boast of having plumage in such a wide range of colours, and with distinctive white cheek-patches set against the brilliant red of its head, neck and breast, a bright yellow belly, a turquoise blue-green rump, red under its tail, sapphire blue wings and a yellow and black patterned back, the Eastern Rosella is as dazzling as any bird could possibly be.

Small groups or pairs of these spectacular birds are often seen on the ground where they eat the seeds of grasses, low-growing shrubs and herbaceous native plants. They're happy to feed in trees too, using one of their feet to grasp their food, with flowers, fruit, nectar and insects all forming part of their varied diet.

Eastern Rosellas, in common with most other Australian parrots, mate for life, and nest in tree hollows, with the female selecting the site and preparing the nesting area. Occasionally a fallen log will be claimed as an alternative residence during the breeding season, but this leaves the birds increasingly vulnerable to attacks by predators, such as foxes and feral and domestic cats and dogs, which have had a devastating impact on the populations of many defenceless ground-dwelling species.

# WATERBIRDS AND WADERS

The world that waterbirds and waders inhabit is full of dangers, and for those that patrol coastal estuaries, tidal mudflats and beaches, the risk of death and injury comes from a silent adversary. The villain that haunts Australia's shores and that hides in the embrace of her oceans is plastic.

Research conducted by the CSIRO (Commonwealth Scientific and Industrial Research Organisation) has revealed that the density of plastic in Australian coastal waters ranges from a few thousand pieces per square kilometre to more than 40,000, while beaches have an average of 11 items of plastic scattered along every metre of sand. Seabirds frequently ingest fragments of plastic that they mistakenly identify as food, and today around half of all seabirds have some plastic in their gut. Many will ultimately die as a result of consuming this carelessly discarded material, and the grim prediction is that by 2050 some 95 per cent of all seabirds will become the victims of plastic. Unless we take action to stem the tide of coastal pollution and reduce the negative impacts that modern lifestyles inflict on the vulnerable creatures with whom we share the planet, we'll have only ourselves to blame when we open our eyes one day and realise that some species have vanished from our shores.

Nankeen Night-Heron near the town of Thargomindah, outback Queensland.

Darter chicks at Bundaberg Botanic Gardens, Queensland.

## AUSTRALIAN DARTER

*Anhinga novaehollandiae*

Anyone who's familiar with the Brazilian Tupi language will be aware that *Anhinga*, the name of the genus to which this bird belongs, means 'snake bird', and when the darter takes to the water, with only its long slender neck visible above the surface, it's easy to see how it acquired its colloquial name of snake-necked darter.

It's a bird that frequents freshwater wetlands, the calm coastal waters of much of the Australian mainland, and lakes in inland regions, and it's often seen beside the water with its wings stretched out to dry.

It has predominantly dark brown to black plumage on its upper body and wings, a long dark tail, a head and long slender neck that's white to grey, a chestnut-brown breast and a long and sharply pointed yellow bill. Females and juveniles can be distinguished by their generally paler plumage.

This large waterbird nibbles on aquatic plants and prowls slowly and stealthily along the water's edge in search of prey that

In flight at Callide Dam, near Biloela, central Queensland.

Darter chicks are covered in white down.

swims into view, the bird's long neck spears through the water and its prey is swiftly and mercilessly impaled on the darter's spear-like bill.

Many waterbirds have waterproof feathers to provide them with increased buoyancy to enable them to float on the surface of the water, but buoyancy is not something that darters require, for they routinely feed on the bottom of shallow streams and lakes, and additional buoyancy would be a hindrance to their aquatic life-style. It's imperative, however, that they dry themselves when they leave the water, and by spreading their large wings out in the sunshine they're also able to regulate their body temperature.

The darter is usually a solitary bird that seeks out others of its kind only when it's nudged into becoming more sociable by the urge to breed. It's usually spring or summer when darters begin to look for a mate, but there is no defined breeding season, and whenever rains fill lakes and streams with water, and food becomes more widely available, it's time for a new cycle of life to begin.

At times, darters nest in colonies with other waterbirds, with cormorants, spoon-bills and ibis being their neighbours, but they often prefer their own company and build their nest in the fork of a tree above the water that will provide all the food they'll need to raise a healthy brood of chicks.

includes insects and crustaceans, but it's in the water that it demonstrates its skills as an efficient predator. With its body submerged and only its head and neck exposed, it hunts for fish, and when a prospective victim

# MAGPIE GOOSE
*Anseranas semipalmata*

It was the mid 20th century when substantial numbers of Magpie Geese were last seen in southern Australia, and today these large birds, thanks to the draining of wetlands, hunting and the impact of droughts, are an endangered species in Victoria and South Australia, and regarded as being vulnerable in New South Wales. Attempts to reintroduce the birds into some areas have had minimal success, but fortunately they're thriving in more northerly parts of the continent, where flocks of

Magpie Geese at Bundaberg Botanic Gardens, Queensland.

hundreds and even thousands of birds are not an uncommon sight.

They inhabit wetlands and floodplains in an area that stretches from the Fitzroy River region of Western Australia, through northern Australia, and along the eastern coast of Queensland, with the birds gradually extending their range down into New South Wales.

The Magpie Goose has black plumage on its long neck and on its head, throat, wings and short tail, with the rest of its feathers being white. It has red skin around its dark eyes, and a red to orange bill. Unlike most other waterbirds, it has clawed toes and only partially webbed feet that, together with its long legs, are bright orange.

These are birds that feed both on land and in the water, but they're relatively fussy characters with only a few plant species making up the major proportion of their diet. They're fairly selective when it comes to choosing a partner too, and they mate for life, with a male usually having two long-term mates, both of which lay their eggs in a shared nest within a colony of breeding birds that's invariably close to wetlands. Each nest, which may be a floating platform of reeds, a simple nest on the ground, or constructed in a tree, may contain as many as a dozen eggs, and the male and his two companions share every aspect of their parental duties, thus giving their chicks the best possible chance of survival.

Magpie Goose in flight at Bundaberg Botanic Gardens, Queensland.

# PLUMED WHISTLING-DUCK

*Dendrocygna eytoni*

The Plumed Whistling-Duck is one of Australia's most beautiful waterbirds, but it doesn't whistle a melodic tune. It simply makes a subtle whistling noise with its wings when in flight.

It's a bird of subtropical and tropical regions that's found across northern Australia and in coastal regions of Queensland and northern New South Wales, where it spends its days in or close to the calm waters of lagoons, lakes and wetlands.

This relatively tall bird is easily recognised by the distinctive cream-coloured plumes of feathers that adorn its sides and that are longer for males than females. It has a light brown head and neck, a back and wings that are a darker brown flecked with cream, a chestnut-coloured breast that's striped with grey, and underparts that are cream with darker stripes. Its bill is a mottled blend of

Male Plumed Whistling-Duck.

Plumed Whistling-Duck at Bundaberg Botanic Gardens, Queensland.

pink and grey, and its legs and feet are pink.

It's a bird that thrives on a diet of grasses and sedges, together with legumes and herbaceous plants that it plucks from the water's edge and from adjacent grasslands, and while the whistling-duck is more than happy to paddle in the water, it rarely dives beneath the surface, and ventures into deep water only when it needs to escape from danger.

Whistling-ducks often congregate in large flocks and share their environment with other waterbirds, but when it's time to breed, each bird knows who its best mate is, for they're strictly monogamous. Their nests are nothing more than shallow depressions in the ground, and from this primitive nursery another generation of these spectacular birds will eventually stride across the landscape to enthral all who see them.

# AUSTRALIAN WOOD DUCK

*Chenonetta jubata*

The Australian Wood Duck is one of a group of aquatic birds that are known as 'dabbling ducks' and that feed near the surface of the water rather than by diving beneath it. They're certainly not averse to getting their feet wet, but they're as much at home on land as they are on the water, and prefer to wade through the shallow and swampy edges of wetlands and streams rather than head out into deep water.

Wood ducks are widespread in Australia, although they're not found in the far northern areas of the continent or in the most arid inland regions. They're quite at home in urban parks that offer adequate sources of food and water, and their diverse range of habitats includes grasslands and woodlands that are adjacent to lakes and waterways, wetlands, calm coastal inlets and farm dams.

A male Australian Wood Duck, with his chocolate-brown head and grey body, speckled brownish-grey breast and black lower belly is a very handsome character indeed, and the female, with her lighter brown head and a white stripe both above and below each eye is most attractive too.

Grasses, clover, sedges and herbaceous plants are the primary ingredients of their natural diet, but they have no hesitation in tucking into the succulent leaves of any cereal crops that may be growing within their range.

They form monogamous pairs and nest in hollows in trees or fallen logs that are close to water, and when they proudly parade across a grassy riverbank with their gaggle of fluffy ducklings in tow, only those with a heart of stone could fail to utter sounds of delight as the family waddles by.

Male Australian Wood Duck at Bundaberg Botanic Gardens, Queensland.

Female Australian Wood Duck.

Adults with ducklings.

# CATTLE EGRET
*Ardea ibis*

O nce upon a time Cattle Egrets strode only across the landscapes of Africa, Europe and Asia, but during the 20th century they discovered the pleasures of global travel. In 1933, a small group of birds was introduced into Western Australia to help control insect pests in cattle grazing areas, and it wasn't long before others arrived under their own steam. The first documented evidence of their unassisted migration was in 1948 when a flock of these elegant white birds was sighted in the Northern Territory, and since then they've established colonies throughout the continent.

Although they can sometimes be seen wading in the shallows of wetlands, Cattle Egrets frequently spend their days feeding well away from any aquatic habitat, and in open woodlands and grasslands they'll enthusiastically feast on grasshoppers and

Cattle Egrets at a nest.

other insects, as well as centipedes, spiders, frogs, earthworms and small lizards. They appreciate company when they dine, and contentedly forage in the company of grazing cattle and other livestock, perching on the backs of the animals that, as they move about, flush insects out of the grass and thus provide the birds with a continual supply of food. Research has revealed that Cattle Egrets feeding in the vicinity of cattle have a 360 per cent greater chance of capturing their prey than when feeding on their own,

but it's not a one-sided relationship, for grazing animals are rewarded as the birds pluck blood-sucking ticks from their skin and feast on swarms of flies.

For much of the year Cattle Egrets have gleaming white plumage, but during the breeding season both males and females put on their most alluring attire and the feathers around each bird's head, neck and chest become vivid orange, and their yellow bills and grey legs become orange too.

They nest in colonies that they often

This is Australia's smallest and most short-billed egret species.

Cattle Egret in breeding plumage.

Breeding-plumaged Cattle Egret feeding its chicks. These images were taken at Bundaberg Botanic Gardens, Queensland.

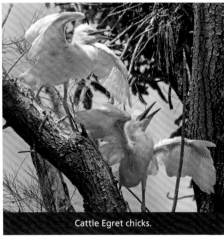

Cattle Egret chicks.

share with other waterbirds, such as Intermediate Egrets and Australian White Ibis, with their nests being simple platforms of sticks in trees that are adjacent to lakes, rivers and wetlands. The chicks are barely two weeks old when they get itchy feet and leave the nest, but at that tender age they're still unable to fly and scramble awkwardly through the treetops. This is a time of great danger for the young and adventurous birds, for death is only one misplaced step away, and for those that tumble from the trees, long-term survival is rarely an option.

This series of images of Intermediate Egrets was taken at Bundaberg Botanic Gardens, Queensland.

## INTERMEDIATE EGRET
*Ardea intermedia*

The elegant Intermediate Egret is at home in most regions of Victoria, New South Wales and Queensland, as well as in the north of Western Australia, the Northern Territory and eastern Tasmania where it inhabits wetlands, flooded grasslands and inland lakes, and is occasionally seen in swampy coastal areas.

With its snow white plumage, a bill that can vary from yellow to black, pale yellow eyes, dark grey legs and a long sinuous neck it's unquestionably a stunning bird. During the breeding season, when both males and females are dressed to impress, the patch of bare skin on its face turns from yellow to green, the base of its bill becomes bright red, and it develops spectacular lacy plumage that drapes across its back and hangs down beyond its tail, and it's then that it earns its alternative common name of 'Plumed Egret.'

The Intermediate Egret is endowed with seemingly limitless patience, at least when hunting for the fish, frogs, crustaceans and insects that are the prime ingredients of its diet. Silently and slowly it prowls in or beside shallow water and stalks its prey, and when the moment is right, it strikes with great speed and snatches its victim from the

water or from the mud in less than the blink of an eye.

As the breeding season gets under way, they form extensive nesting colonies with other waterbirds as their neighbours, and lay their eggs in ramshackle nests of sticks in the trees that hem wetlands. Many, when their chicks have fledged, migrate to other regions, with some heading south to Tasmania, while others undertake a more adventurous journey to New Zealand or New Guinea, but when the breeding season approaches once again, they return to their familiar breeding grounds.

Pacific Gull on the beach at Baird Bay on the Eyre Peninsula, South Australia.

# PACIFIC GULL

*Larus pacificus*

The Pacific Gull only occasionally visits Australia's Pacific coast, and although it can be seen as far north as Sydney, it's most likely to be spotted where the Southern and Indian Oceans lap at the beaches of Tasmania, and in southern coastal regions of the mainland.

There are two subspecies of this attractive bird, which is the largest Australian gull. The eastern Pacific Gull, which is found on the south-eastern coast and in Tasmania, spends its days patrolling sheltered sandy beaches, paddling in the shallow waters of river estuaries, and bobbing on the calm waters of harbours, while the western subspecies has a preference for more exposed and rocky sections of the coast and adjacent islands.

With its distinctive yellow bill, black back, black wings tipped with white, black tail, white head and underparts and yellow legs, the Pacific Gull is very handsome. Those that live in south-eastern regions and that have a white eye-patch and a completely red tip to their bill are just as good looking as their western relatives that have a red eye and merely a small red patch on the tip of the bill. Juveniles, although they're very distinctive in their mottled grey to brown plumage, don't don the more attractive dress of maturity until they're approximately four years of age.

Pacific Gulls could never be accused of being fastidious eaters, for they're happy to feast on small fish and squid, crustaceans and the scraps discarded by fishermen, and if such a varied diet isn't enough to satisfy their appetite, they'll raid the nests of other birds and devour unguarded eggs and chicks.

In their coastal habitat they're never thirsty, for they can drink salt water with no adverse effects, thanks to special glands that extract any excess salt, which is then excreted through the bird's nostrils. When a Pacific Gull shakes its head vigorously, it's merely removing any build up of salt from its bill.

In the breeding season birds come together in colonies on isolated headlands and islands where they create their simple nests, with some females content to lay their eggs in nothing more than a stony depression in the ground, while others create a more deluxe version using grass, sticks and seaweed.

Camouflaged juvenile Pacific Gull near Streaky Bay on the Eyre Peninsula, South Australia.

White-faced Heron on the beach at Hervey Bay, Queensland.

## WHITE-FACED HERON

*Egretta novaehollandiae*

Wherever there's water there's a good chance that the aptly named White-faced Heron won't be far away, for it makes itself at home in a wide range of habitats throughout the continent, and is often spotted strolling across tidal mudflats and beaches and wading through the shallow waters that hem river estuaries. Australia's most common and widespread heron is a regular visitor to both coastal and inland wetlands and is often seen meandering across wet grasslands and pastures, and this distinctive bird doesn't hesitate to drop into urban parklands if there's a source of water offering the hint that a free banquet.

In addition to eating fish, eels and crustaceans, White-faced Herons also feast on frogs, small reptiles, rodents and insects. They generally dine alone, and although they'll often do little more than stand and wait patiently for prey to come their way, they also employ more energetic tactics to snatch a meal. They prowl slowly through the water, stirring it with their feet to flush aquatic creatures out of their hiding places, and make a frenetic dash, with their wings outstretched, in pursuit of any edible creature that attempts to escape their predatory attentions.

These are attractive birds with predominantly blue-grey plumage and, as their name suggests, white faces. Each has a long, slender neck, a long dark grey bill and long yellow legs, and as pairs contemplate breeding, they develop brownish-grey feathers, known as nuptial plumes, on the head, neck and back.

White-faced Herons generally breed in southern Australia, and are the only herons that breed in Tasmania, and although they usually settle down to start a family in spring, they'll enthusiastically take advantage of rainfall that may fill ephemeral lakes and replenish streams and waterholes and bring with it an increase in the populations of the aquatic creatures that provide the birds with food.

Their nests are primitive and scruffy structures made of sticks that are placed on a branch of a tree overhanging water to ensure that food is on hand for the growing family. When the chicks have finally fledged, the elegant White-faced Herons make their way back to their favoured habitats around the county, habitats that are frequently on the doorstep of cities and towns.

In flight at Fraser Island, Queensland.

White-faced Heron on the beach at Hervey Bay, Queensland.

Juvenile Nankeen Night-Heron wading in a bore drain at Yowah, outback Queensland.

# NANKEEN NIGHT-HERON
*Nycticorax caledonicus*

In Australia's colonial era, early settlers used a Chinese fabric called nankeen to make some of their clothes. It had the same cinnamon-brown colour as the feathers of the heron that was frequently seen around permanent sources of water, so to distinguish this bird from other heron species it was given a common name that made it instantly recognisable. It became known as the Nankeen Night-Heron.

Fortunately, it's not essential to be out and about in the dark to see this distinctive bird in its natural habitat, for despite its name it's not a strictly nocturnal species. Woodlands and forests on the banks of waterways, lakes, coastal estuaries and freshwater swamps throughout mainland Australia are its favoured haunts, and it's occasionally seen in similar environments in Tasmania. During daylight hours, particularly in overcast or wet weather, the Nankeen Night-Heron may be out and about searching for food, but when it's not stealthily hunting its prey, it settles down to take life easy and dozes among the foliage of a tree at the water's edge.

There's often some confusion about the identification of this attractive bird, for it wears two distinctly different costumes. The feathers on the back and wings of an adult are the cinnamon-brown colour that led to the bird's common name. The lower parts of its body and its neck are creamy-brown, its face is white, its bill is grey, the crown of its head is black and it has yellow eyes, legs and feet. Juveniles bear little resemblance to their parents, for their entire body and head are draped with plumage in decorative patterns that are a mixture of light brown, dark brown and white streaks. As they mature they gradually develop the black cap worn by adults, but the rest of their plumage remains streaked and mottled until they reach full adulthood.

Droughts, the decline of wetlands and the interruption of river flows have had a dramatic impact on populations of Nankeen Night-Herons, for they thrive only in areas where there's a permanent source of water that ensures that their favourite foods are right on the doorstep. They become increasingly active at dusk, and feed in shallow water where, as they probe the mud with their long pointed bills, they catch small crustaceans, fish, frogs and aquatic insects, and occasionally they satisfy their hunger by eating the

Juvenile Nankeen Night-Heron beside Wallam Creek at Bollon, outback Queensland.

Nankeen Night-Heron near Thargomindah, outback Queensland.

eggs and small chicks of other birds.

When it's time to start thinking of raising a family, breeding birds reveal their intentions by developing two or three long, narrow white feathers that adorn their heads. Males busy themselves by collecting nesting material, while females create a simple platform of twigs in a tree that overhangs the water and that's often among a colony of other nesting birds, including egrets and cormorants.

It might require a little patience to discover a Nankeen Night-Heron as it sits, perfectly camouflaged, in its daytime retreat, but any glimpse of this stunning bird, young or old, male or female, in whatever attractive dress it might be wearing, is guaranteed to provide a memorable experience.

Adult Australian White Ibis.

## AUSTRALIAN WHITE IBIS
*Threskiornis molucca*

Religion played a major role in the lives of ancient Egyptians who regarded many creatures, including the ibis, as sacred, so it was only logical that early ornithologists should give the genus to which this bird belongs a name that adequately reflected its status. *Threskiornis*, from the Greek words *threskos*, meaning 'sacred', and *ornis*, meaning 'bird', was the moniker with which they christened it.

The body and wings of the Australian White Ibis, surprise, surprise, are predominantly white, but a bare black head and neck, tuft of cream plumes at the base of the neck, long curved bill and vivid red patches under the wings guarantee that this large and elegant bird stands out from the crowd.

This is a species that's widespread in northern and eastern areas of mainland Australia, with isolated populations thriving in the south-western corner of the continent where, for aeons, the birds have been content to inhabit areas adjacent to coastal

Note the red 'wing-pits' in flight.

more than muddy puddles and cracked soil in their wake, large populations of this ibis are forced to find somewhere new to call home. In recent decades they've discovered inviting alternative habitats with permanent sources of water and ample supplies of food, and have enthusiastically taken up residence in urban areas and in woodlands that hem the waterways that slice through cities and towns.

They've proved to be extremely adaptable, and their diet reflects that adaptability. It includes a wide range of aquatic prey, such as insects, fish, frogs, yabbies, other small crustaceans and mussels that the birds discover while wading through shallow water and probing the mud with their long bills. They dine in agricultural areas too, and are welcome visitors, thanks to their voracious appetites for grasshoppers, locusts and other insects, and although these imposing birds are invaluable warriors that are on the side of farmers in their perpetual battle to control insect pests, not everyone is happy to have them on their doorstep, and in urban areas it's the birds themselves that are often regarded as pests.

Large populations have become permanent squatters in parklands where they pollute the water of ornamental lakes and create an overpowering stench. They're more than happy to scoff bread and other handouts provided by well-meaning humans, they incessantly scrounge for food

and freshwater wetlands, tidal estuaries and shallow lakes, but the environment is continually changing, and the ibis have taken the changes in their stride.

Water is an essential component of any habitat that can support them, and during periods of drought, when shallow lakes and streams have vanished and left nothing at outdoor cafes and in popular picnic areas, and they scavenge for scraps in rubbish tips in such huge numbers that they're disparagingly referred to as 'rubbish dump chooks' and 'tip turkeys'. Although it's difficult to accurately assess the population of urban ibis, there are believed to be in excess of 5,700 birds in Sydney alone, with the city's major rubbish tip visited by some 800 birds every day.

When the breeding season arrives, immense flocks settle in trees adjacent to water and construct their nests, which are little more than untidy platforms of sticks. They share their huge colonies with other bird species, and chaos reigns as the mayhem of raising chicks gets into full swing and adults, bearing gifts of food, are relentlessly coming and going among the tangled mass of nests, which are often crammed so close together that it's hard to distinguish where one ends and another begins.

With climate change predicted to punish the Australian landscape with more frequent and more prolonged periods of drought, ibis will be in no hurry to abandon the easy life that they've discovered in Australia's sprawling cities and suburbs. With females laying up to three clutches of eggs each season and individuals living for at least two decades, these majestic birds, which are either adored or despised, will remain on the doorstep of millions of people for many years to come.

Australian White Ibis in parklands at Maryborough, Queensland.

Nest at Bundaberg Botanic Gardens, Queensland.

Australian Pied Oystercatchers on a beach in New South Wales.

# AUSTRALIAN PIED OYSTERCATCHER

*Haematopus longirostris*

This distinctive oystercatcher – one of only five Australian shorebird species that nest exclusively on or close to the beach – can often be seen strolling along sandy shores and dabbling in the mud of estuaries all around the Australian coast, although it's regarded as an endangered species in New South Wales.

The rough translation of its scientific name is 'blood foot and long nose,' and what could be a more apt description of the Australian Pied Oystercatcher's most conspicuous physical features? Its head,

neck, back and wings are black, and its underparts are white, but with a long red bill and blood red eyes and legs, it's a bird of particularly striking appearance.

Despite their common name, these coastal birds rarely tuck into oysters that thrive on rocky shores, for they prefer to spend their days on sandy beaches or mudflats where they search for marine worms, crabs and molluscs that they prise open with bills that are specially adapted for the task. Occasionally, when they're eager for a change of taste, they forage among rocks for other shellfish that they skilfully remove from their algae-cloaked retreats.

The Australian Pied Oystercatcher, a shy bird that likes to keep its distance

Australian Pied Oystercatcher on the beach at Bournda National Park, New South Wales.

from humans, is usually seen alone, with its mate or in a small group. Despite its stark colouration it's surprisingly well camouflaged during the breeding season when the female settles down in a nest that's little more than a depression in the sand. She and her mate vigorously defend their nesting site and use some cunning tactics to divert predators away from their vulnerable chicks, with one of the birds fluttering away from the nest with a wing dragging along the ground in an attempt to demonstrate that it's injured and thus incapable of flight. With the attentions of a potential enemy diverted from the nest, the bird can eventually return to its parental duties, but if the ruse fails, both birds will aggressively attack the intruder and reinforce the message that Australian Pied Oystercatcher chicks are definitely not on the menu.

Nesting Australian Pied Oystercatcher.

Black-fronted Dotterel at Eungalla Dam, beside a popular camping area in northern Queensland.

Reflected in the muddy water of an outback waterhole near Thargomindah, Queensland.

## BLACK-FRONTED DOTTEREL
*Elseyornis melanops*

The Black-fronted Dotterel is often referred to as a 'guttersnipe', but with the Oxford Dictionary defining the word as 'a young, uncared for and mischievous child' it's a peculiar name for a bird that invariably displays neat and clean plumage, and that never seems to be getting into any mischief, other than dabbling about in a little mud.

This attractive little bird can be seen in most regions of Australia, but tends to shun the most arid parts of the continent, and although it's occasionally spotted wandering beside saline mudflats and coastal estuaries, its favoured habitats are freshwater wetlands, the stony beds of rivers and creeks, the muddy edges of lakes, and the shallow

Black-fronted Dotterel near a camp site in outback Queensland.

pools of water that laze in outback claypans.

The Black-fronted Dotterel has some very distinctive features, including a black and white head, white chin and white breast with a black stripe. Its legs are pink to orange, its bill is bright red with a black tip, and its dark eyes are ringed with red. With decoratively patterned brown plumage on its back and wings, this diminutive bird is another vivid example of Mother Nature's unrivalled artistic skills.

These birds spend their days alone or with a mate, and are energetic characters that are fascinating to watch as they go about the routine task of searching for the insects and small aquatic creatures that form the basis of their diet. At times they dawdle across the soft mud at the water's edge, then rush quickly and silently along, rather than flying in pursuit of a mobile snack. They stop momentarily to peck at the mud, and in their hunt for food they scurry on their way again at a pace that continually alternates between short bursts of speed and a leisurely stroll as they peck repetitively at the ground.

Their plumage provides them with excellent camouflage, and when they settle down on their nests that are usually close to water and are often little more than shallow depressions in the ground, they're almost impossible to see. As a predominantly ground-dwelling species, the Black-fronted Dotterel is particularly vulnerable to predation by feral cats and foxes, and with many wetlands and shallow lakes drying up during repetitive droughts, some populations of these delightful little birds are in decline.

Pelicans on an island near Mallacoota, Victoria.

# AUSTRALIAN PELICAN
*Pelecanus conspicillatus*

It takes a plethora of adjectives to accurately describe the Australian Pelican, for it's a friendly, inquisitive, beautiful and elegant bird.

Pelicans have been part of Australia's wildlife community for millions of years, and today, with a population of 300,000–500,000, they're found wherever there's water, from the coast to the most remote corners of the outback.

They inhabit beaches and estuaries, and are regular visitors to harbours and wharfs where they plead for fishermen's scraps and fight among themselves to snatch whatever treats are tossed their way. They drift on the calm waters of lakes, wade in the shallows of saline and freshwater wetlands and stroll across the lawns of urban parklands that border meandering rivers.

When heavy rains inundate the outback and vast and arid saltpans are transformed into sparkling blue lakes, thousands of pelicans head inland to breed, and in 1990, when floodwaters filled Lake Eyre in northern South Australia, some 100,000 birds raised an estimated 90,000 chicks at the water's edge. When the waters of inland lakes ultimately evaporate and the good times and an abundance of food come to an end, the birds return to their familiar haunts where permanent supplies of food and water are guaranteed.

Pelicans are one of the heaviest flying birds in the world, and while taking off from the water requires considerable effort, once airborne these great birds, with a wingspan of up to 2.5m, can glide and soar effortlessly for long periods of time. Although they routinely fly at altitudes of 1,000m, pelicans have been recorded soaring at heights of 3,000m.

The Australian Pelican has a white head, neck and underparts, black back, black and white wings, short tail and yellow skin around the eyes. Its most distinguishing feature however is its huge bill and the attached pouch that, with its extreme sensitivity, allows the bird to locate its prey even in the murkiest of water. Although pelicans often feed alone, their great success as predators comes when they work together as a group, known as a pod or squadron, and either swim in formation to surround their prey or herd fish or crustaceans into shallow water. When a meal is within their reach, the birds plunge their bills into the water, using their pouches as nets to scoop up their catch.

Pelicans are highly social birds, and never more so than when they're ready to breed, for they nest in colonies that are often populated by thousands of birds, with each

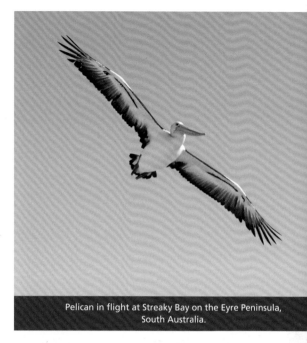
Pelican in flight at Streaky Bay on the Eyre Peninsula, South Australia.

Pelican at Tuncurry, New South Wales.

Australian Pelican at Cooper Creek at Innamincka, outback South Australia.

Australian Pelican with plastic waste in its bill at Baird Bay on the Eyre Peninsula, South Australia.

nest being merely a hollow in the sand or among vegetation at the water's edge.

Life wasn't meant to be easy for young pelicans, and if their parents feel threatened they simply abandon their nest, leaving their chicks to a grim fate. Those that survive eventually congregate with other fledglings, and they wait impatiently for their parents to return from fishing trips with the welcome meals that will sustain the young birds until they're ready to fly and to fend for themselves.

Australian Pelicans at Cooper Creek at Innamincka, outback South Australia.

Royal Spoonbills beside a caravan park at Scott's Head, New South Wales.

## ROYAL SPOONBILL
*Platalea regia*

Although it's rarely seen in Tasmania and is regarded as a vulnerable species in Victoria, the Royal Spoonbill is found in most other regions of the continent, with the exception of south-western and central Australia. It thrives in a great diversity of habitats, with its primary demand being shallow water, and that means that this majestic character is frequently a resident of freshwater and saltwater wetlands, tidal mudflats and lakes. Its dazzling white plumage contrasts dramatically with its large black bill and long black legs, and although this regal bird needs no feature other than its uniquely shaped bill to make it a most distinctive creature, just for good measure it has black facial skin with a yellow patch above each eye, and a red patch on its forehead. During the breeding season it develops long plumes on the back of its head, which are raised during mating displays.

This is a bird that, when foraging for food, takes life at a leisurely pace. It wades slowly through the water, shuffling along

Royal Spoonbill with nuptial plumes in Bundaberg Botanic Gardens, Queensland.

to stir up the sediment with its feet and sending any prospective prey scurrying for safety, but even in murky water the small fish, aquatic insects, crustaceans and frogs that are the main ingredients of the bird's diet have little hope of escape.

The spoon-shaped section of its bill is the perfect tool for this aquatic bird, for the sensors, called papillae, on the inside of the bill allow the bird to sense the slightest movement of its prey. Once it's aware that some tasty morsel is in the vicinity, it sweeps its bill slowly back and forth in a wide arc through the water to grab any small and tasty creatures that are within its reach.

Royal Spoonbills spend much of their lives alone, but when they're ready to breed each seeks out a mate and the pair set up home in a colony that's shared with other birds, including ibis, herons and egrets. In a tree that's close to water, or among a dense forest of reeds, the birds construct their bowl-shaped nests from twigs, and line them with foliage and aquatic vegetation, or simply renovate one that has been used in previous years.

When the hullabaloo of mating and nest building has died down, Royal Spoonbills appreciate a little peace and quiet, and if they're disturbed, a nesting pair, or even the entire colony, may abandon their eggs and head to an environment where the safety and the solitude that they demand are assured.

Royal Spoonbill on nest in Bundaberg Botanic Gardens, Queensland.

Royal Spoonbill beside a caravan park at Scott's Head, New South Wales.

Whimbrel on the beach at Iluka, New South Wales.

## WHIMBREL

*Numenius phaeopus*

Whimbrels arrive on Australia's shores each year after an epic journey from their breeding grounds in Siberia, Alaska and other subarctic regions. Tagged birds have been recorded flying continuously for six days on a journey covering a distance of 7,000km at an average speed of 46km/h, but their long flight through the skies above east and south-east Asia, on what's referred to as the East Asian / Australasian Flyway, is fraught with danger.

Up to 2 million birds, including an estimated 100,000 Whimbrels, use the route every year, and it's the human race that bears the responsibility for one of the most serious risks that these avian travellers face on their arduous trek. The Yellow Sea, an extensive inlet of the Pacific Ocean that stretches between mainland China and the Korean Peninsula and that, for aeons, has been the habitat of many species of aquatic wildlife, is a major stopover point for many migratory birds. They rest and recuperate on its shores, and feed in the intertidal zone and in the sea's relatively shallow waters, but the environment is changing at an alarming pace and the degradation of this vital habitat makes the birds' difficult journey more hazardous every year.

During the last 50–100 years, approximately 40 per cent of the intertidal area that borders the Yellow Sea has been reclaimed for development, and with reclamation continuing at a rapid rate, and the additional threat from water that's polluted by industrial chemicals, agricultural runoff and sewage, the future for migratory shorebirds such as the Whimbrel appears to be increasingly grim.

The first Whimbrels to touch down on Australian soil generally arrive in August. The majority remain on the northern coast of the continent, but some move inland and are occasionally seen wading in shallow saline lakes. Their itchy feet gradually lead these global travellers to the edges of the continent where they make themselves at home in sheltered coastal areas of Queensland, Western Australia and New South Wales, with some flying as far south as Victoria, South Australia and Tasmania.

This relatively large wading bird has dark brown wings streaked with cream, a similarly coloured back, a lighter brown head that's also streaked with cream and that has a dark brown to black crown, underparts that are cream to white and mottled with dark brown, and a long curved dark grey bill that is the Whimbrel's most distinguishing feature.

Any coastal environment where food, such as marine worms, crustaceans and small fish, is guaranteed is a prime habitat for these distinctive birds, and shallow lagoons, intertidal mudflats and river estuaries, particularly those that are cloaked with mangroves, are where Whimbrels prefer to dine. As each day comes to its inevitable conclusion, they settle down to roost among the branches of mangrove trees or on artificial structures that, at high tide, are isolated from the land and from any potential predators.

As the summer months pass, Whimbrels instinctively know that it's time to be on the move once again, and they increase their feeding activities in anticipation of the long journey that lies ahead. In February they begin to head north, and by the end of April, the glimpse of a Whimbrel on Australian shores is only a pleasant memory of the past or a dream of the future.

Brolga in a dry riverbed at Boulia, outback Queensland.

## BROLGA

*Grus rubicunda*

According to Aboriginal legend there was a beautiful young girl named Buralga who loved to dance. She sealed her fate when she rejected the amorous attentions of an evil sorcerer, for in revenge he changed her into a bird, and today this eye-catching and graceful creature dances across the Australian landscape.

The Brolga is the official bird emblem of Queensland and is featured on the state's coat of arms, and although it's primarily a resident of northern and north-eastern Australia, it also inhabits semi-arid inland regions of the continent that stretch as far south as central New South Wales and western Victoria.

These imposing birds generally live close to water, and make themselves at home in areas where wetlands, coastal mudflats, grassy plains and irrigated farmlands are on the doorstep. With a population of 20,000–100,000, they're a prolific species, but with the continual destruction of their habitat and the predation of eggs and chicks by foxes and feral cats, their numbers, particularly in the southern extremity of their range, are in decline.

Brolgas, which stand almost 2m high, have light grey plumage with black tips to their wings, long slender necks and long legs, long grey bills and golden-yellow eyes. Their most distinctive feature however, is the vivid red skin that covers the head, with the exception of the grey crown, as well as the cheeks and throat.

They typically spend their days with a mate, in a small family group or, during the non-breeding season, as members of a large flock, and although each is a picture of elegance as it strides across the landscape, it's when a Brolga takes to the skies that this iconic creature, with its wingspan of more than 2m, presents a spectacular aerial performance that's as mesmerising as its terrestrial dance.

Brolgas are as happy in wetlands as flying-foxes in an orchard of ripening mangoes, for it's here that they forage for a range of foods that includes tubers and roots, succulent leaves, crustaceans and frogs. If that's not enough to satisfy their appetite, they'll also tuck into cereal grains and other seeds, and scoff insects and small lizards. As they wade through the shallows of saline swamps they have no qualms about drinking the water, for they excrete excess salt through special glands near their eyes.

They are among the most entertaining of Mother Nature's diverse cast of performers, and their most enthralling display begins when one or more birds takes the first steps in a complex dance routine. During the first act, a bird plucks some grass from the ground, tosses it into the air and, while dancing, catches it in its bill. Then, with its great wings outstretched, it continues the dance, jumping into the air, bowing gracefully, and bobbing its head up and down to the accompaniment of a repertoire of calls. These are monogamous birds that usually share their lives with the same mate every year, and although a single bird may perform to impress its partner, several will often dance together in an entrancing performance that can be seen at any time of the year, but that's also part of a courtship ritual.

It's usually rain that triggers the urge to mate, and the happy couple establish their nesting territory in a wetland area that offers a reliable supply of food. They may take the lazy option and use the abandoned nest of a swan, or simply lay their eggs on bare ground, but those that want the best for their chicks create a nest that's merely a pile of sticks, grass and other plant material on any soil that protrudes, like a miniature island, from the surface of shallow water.

Brolga in flight at Boulia, outback Queensland.

The protective parents know all the tricks to protect their chicks, and in the face of imminent danger they distract a predator by fluttering across the ground as though suffering from an injury, and thus lure the threatening creature away from the chicks that the pair continues to protect until they're ready to breed again.

# BIRDS OF PREY AND OWLS

## WEDGE-TAILED EAGLE
*Aquila audax*

The Wedge-tailed Eagle, Australia's largest bird of prey and the fourth largest eagle in the world, has a scientific name that means 'bold eagle', and it can afford to be bold, for this majestic creature rules both the sky and the land, with only humans threatening its supremacy.

It's this great bird's indomitable courage and a dogged determination to defend its territory against any perceived threat that occasionally sees it attack hang gliders, ultra light aircraft and drones. Although many birds tremble at the mere glimpse of a Wedge-tailed Eagle, some species, including magpies, butcherbirds and Noisy Miners, are unintimidated by its presence and, in a defiant David and Goliath scene, will aggressively attack when one of these giants of the skies arrives in their neighbourhood.

The Tasmanian subspecies, *Aquila audax fleayi*, with less than 200 pairs surviving in the wild, is listed as endangered, but in mainland Australia the future of the Wedge-tailed Eagle is secure. They can frequently be seen perched on dead trees or power

Wedge-tailed Eagle at an Aboriginal settlement in outback Queensland.

Wedge-tailed Eagle at an Aboriginal settlement in outback Queensland.

Wedge-tailed Eagle at an Aboriginal settlement in outback Queensland.

Wedge-tailed Eagle near Woomera, outback South Australia.

poles, feeding on roadside carrion, or soaring effortless through the skies above their widespread and varied habitats that range from coastal areas to arid inland regions.

Young eagles have brown plumage with lighter chestnut-brown feathers on their wings and head. Their colouration becomes darker as they age, with adults usually being predominantly dark brown or almost black, and all have a dense covering of feathers on their legs and a long wedge-shaped tail.

This great eagle is a spectacular sight in any situation, but when in flight its display of elegance ensures that anyone fortunate enough to be a spectator will be begging for an encore. With a wingspan of up to 2.3m, these magnificent raptors can soar for hours and drift and twirl across the sky in aerial displays as, on the invisible hands of breezes, they're carried high above the Earth for the best bird's eye view imaginable. Three of these majestic birds, with their flight monitored by tiny transmitters, were recently recorded soaring at altitudes of up to 6.5km above Western Australia – and the only explanation for their adventure is that they were simply having fun.

These mighty birds of prey are despised by many farmers and graziers for their crimes of killing lambs, and although Wedge-tailed Eagles are undoubtedly guilty as charged, it's usually only animals that are weak or injured that fall victim to these highly efficient predators. There's plenty of other food available for these imposing carnivores and they prey on a wide range of native animals, including small kangaroos and wallabies, possums and bandicoots, birds, reptiles and rodents, but in areas where large populations of rabbits thrive, these introduced animals account for around 70 per cent of a Wedge-tailed Eagle's diet, and that makes them heroes in the continual struggle to reduce populations of these unwelcome feral pests.

Wedge-tailed Eagles offer the environment a helping hand in other ways too, for they routinely take the easy dining option and feast on carrion, and with collisions between wildlife and vehicles, together with repetitive droughts, ensuring that the landscape, particularly in outback regions, is littered with the carcasses of kangaroos and other wild creatures, these great birds never feel the pangs of hunger. From a long distance away they can easily spot the activity of crows or other raptors that have gathered around a carcass, and with the primary rule at Mother Nature's dinner table being that the largest birds are in charge, the eagles invariably get first peck at the feast. Up to 20 may descend on a single corpse, but with a strict pecking order enforced, only two or three feed, while others wait impatiently for their turn or squabble among themselves to be next in line to gorge themselves at the banquet.

Wedge-tailed Eagles mate for life, and as the breeding season approaches, pairs

Wedge-tailed Eagle near a camping area in outback Queensland.

Wedge-tailed Eagle feeding on kangaroo carcass near the outback town of Oodnadatta, South Australia.

perform dramatic aerial displays, and eventually settle down to renovate a previously used nest or to create a new platform of sticks in the fork of a tall tree from where they have an uninterrupted view of the surrounding landscape.

Land clearing practices have dramatically reduced the number of nesting sites that are available for these large raptors.

Many birds have been shot by landowners who see them as a threat to their livestock, and eagles continue to die as a result of eating poisoned baits that have been widely distributed to control populations of feral dogs and pigs. The good news is that these awe-inspiring raptors are thriving, and will continue to put on their stunning performances for many years to come.

# PACIFIC BAZA
*Aviceda subcristata*

This glorious raptor's name might sound a little strange, but with the knowledge that *baz*, a word within the Hindi language, refers to a goshawk, there's some rationale behind the bird's name, for it bears a considerably resemblance to the Australian Brown Goshawk.

The Pacific Baza has predominantly grey plumage on its wings, head, neck and upper breast, a dark brown back, chestnut-brown rear underparts and a long dark grey tail. It has a hooked bill for tearing at its prey, short legs with long and viciously sharp talons and brilliant golden-yellow eyes, but two other attractive characteristics make it easy to identify. It has a dark grey crest on the back of its head, a feature that gives it the alternative common name of 'Crested Hawk', and its chest is adorned with feathers in wide brown and cream horizontal stripes.

The hunting grounds of Pacific Bazas are generally in the treetops, and although they may spend long periods of time perching silently among the foliage and scanning the area around them for any signs of prey, they're not slow to react when they spot something of interest, and will fly low and silently above or through the forest or woodland canopy, and dive, with talons extended, to pluck a victim from the trees or from the air. Small mammals, reptiles and the chicks of other birds form part of their diet, as do native fruits, but it's large grasshoppers, stick insects, praying mantids and frogs that they find irresistible.

Pacific Baza in the author's garden.

Pacific Bazas at a bird bath in the author's garden.

For much of the year, usually from early winter to the middle of spring, they travel widely through their range, which includes the tropical and subtropical forests and woodlands of northern and eastern Australia, but they rarely venture south of Sydney. This seasonal movement is believed to be in response to the availability of food that, in some sectors of their habitat, may be reduced during the coldest months of the year.

Smaller birds are far from impressed when these imposing raptors move into their territory and, like a mob of vigilantes, some

will persistently harass Pacific Bazas and do their best to persuade them to move elsewhere. They're rarely intimidated however, and stoically ignore the aggressive antics of the neighbourhood watch brigade, and only move on when, as summer approaches, they have more than food on their minds.

In the breeding season they relocate to riverine woodlands and rainforests where, in the high branches of trees, they build their fragile nests of sticks, lay their eggs, and patiently await the arrival of the next generation of one of Australia's most attractive birds of prey.

Brahminy Kite on the beach at the city of Hervey Bay, Queensland.

## BRAHMINY KITE
*Haliastur indus*

The Brahminy Kite's range extends from South Asia to Australia. It spreads its wings over India where it's revered as the sacred bird that carried the Hindu deity Lord Vishnu to the heavens, but in Indonesia it's a symbol of the modern era, for this majestic bird has been adopted as the official emblem of the city of Jakarta and represents the government's commitment to the protection of wildlife.

If legends are to be believed, the Brahminy Kite was born on the island of Bougainville, and the tale of its birth begins with a mother who left her baby under a banana tree while working in her garden. The crying infant floated up into the sky and was miraculously transformed into a bird, with the child's necklace becoming the Brahminy Kite's colourful feathers.

It's easy to see why this stunning raptor is so highly revered, for its undeniable beauty casts a momentary spell over all who see it, and in Australia it can be sighted in the northern coastal regions of Western Australia and the Northern Territory, and south through Queensland to northern New South Wales. Although it typically frequents mangrove swamps, tidal mudflats and river estuaries, it's also occasionally seen

Brahminy Kite over the ocean waves at Iluka, New South Wales.

around inland wetlands and waterways.

The Brahminy Kite has a white head and breast, with the plumage on the rest of its body being a golden-brown. It has short pale yellow legs with massive needle-sharp talons, and a pale yellow hooked bill.

This magnificent bird of prey is an unrivalled hunter that glides effortlessly over its territory and dives down to a river or the ocean to skilfully snatch fish from beneath the surface. It will grab small birds from among the trees, and adds reptiles, insects and rodents to its diet whenever they come within its gaze, but the Brahminy Kite is also a scavenger. It feeds on dead fish and crustaceans that may have been washed up on the beach, scoffs scraps discarded by fishermen, and has no qualms about harassing other fish-eating birds to such a degree that they're forced to abandon their meal and flee from the unwelcome attentions of this large and dominant predator.

Brahminy Kites are generally solitary birds, except during the breeding season. Their nests, which are usually in trees close to water, can be massive platforms of sticks that are reused for several years, and after making some renovations, with the addition of a few twigs or pieces of driftwood, all the birds need to do is to line the nest with lichen or seaweed, and lay a clutch of eggs from which a new generation of these glorious birds will eventually emerge into the world.

Whistling Kite is distinctive in flight due to the pale patch in the middle of the otherwise dark flight feathers.

## WHISTLING KITE

*Haliastur sphenurus*

Whistling Kites, which have light brown to cream plumage with darker brown streaks on the head, breast and the under side of the tail, and dark brown wings, can be found throughout Australia, although they're rarely seen in Tasmania.

With their distinctive whistling voice, they're usually heard before they're seen in their prime habitats that include wetlands and both open country and lightly wooded areas that are in close proximity to water.

Whistling Kites will hunt for live prey or scavenge for carrion.

other birds, small mammals, grasshoppers and yabbies, and when live prey is scarce, or if they're feeling rather lethargic, they'll happily dine on carrion.

Whistling Kites congregate around areas that are at the mercy of bushfires, and wild creatures that have survived the flames face another fate in the talons of these skilful avian hunters that will savagely harass other predatory birds that have already caught their prey, forcing them to abandon a meal that the kites then steal with no hint of hesitation.

Despite the fact that both sexes have similar plumage the female, in common with other species of raptors, is larger and more imposing than her mate. In the case of the Whistling Kite the difference is quite considerable however, with the female being around 20 per cent larger than the male and a whopping 40 per cent heavier.

They form large flocks only when there's an abundance of food, with these beautiful raptors preferring to spend their lives alone or with a lifelong mate. Each pair usually creates a nest, which is little more than a platform of sticks covered with a layer of leaves, in the fork of a high tree that's close to water, and will vigorously defend their nesting site against any intruders. With two or three clutches of eggs laid each year, this majestic kite will be whistling throughout Australia well into the foreseeable future.

They whistle when perching on the branches of trees, and they whistle when they're soaring gracefully high above the ground or the water in search of their prey, which includes rabbits, fish, reptiles, the chicks of

Juvenile Barking Owl in the author's garden.

## BARKING OWL
*Ninox connivens*

Anyone who has heard the distinctive call of the Barking Owl needs no imagination to comprehend the reason behind the name of this nocturnal bird of prey, for the repetitive *woof woof* that reverberates across the landscape perfectly mimics the sound of a barking dog.

Early European settlers heard the bird's calls too, and they also heard Aboriginal tales of the legendary bunyip that emerged from its lair in waterholes and swamps to feast on women, and bloodcurdling screams that occasionally shattered the silence of the night gave some credence to the story. The sound, however, was nothing more than the eerie alarm call of the Barking Owl, which is also known as the 'screaming woman owl.'

The extensive range of the Barking Owl includes eastern, northern and south-western regions of the Australian mainland where it inhabits forests and woodlands that are dominated by either eucalyptus or melaleuca trees. They are also found in southern areas of the continent, but their population in this region has declined

Above and opposite: Barking Owl in a hollow tree at Coongie Lakes National Park, outback South Australia.

considerably in past years, due primarily to land clearing and the subsequent reduction in the number of old trees with hollows that the birds require for their daytime roosts and nesting sites. The Barking Owl is a vulnerable species in New South Wales but has fared far worse in Victoria where it is the state's most threatened owl and is listed as an endangered species.

Adults have brown wings with white spots, cream and brown vertical streaks on the chest, and a brown to grey head, with similarly coloured plumage surrounding their large yellow eyes and the bill that's yellow with a black tip.

The bird's call, which often begins at dusk, is believed to be a warning to other birds that may be encroaching on the territory. Its frightening scream is intended to terrify any creatures that may threaten it, and the subdued sounds that the male emits during the breeding season are merely to alert its partner to the fact that he has arrived with food.

These highly efficient hunters have a varied diet and will take prey from the ground, from trees, or from the surface of water, and will even capture flying creatures in mid-air. Whatever they can carry in their long talons is fair game, and that includes birds as large as magpies, rabbits, rodents, insects and reptiles, and other creatures such as possums, gliders and bats that, like the Barking Owl, are out and about during the night.

During daylight hours the Barking Owl roosts in large trees on the edges of waterways and wetlands, often in a sheltered hollow within the tree's trunk or gnarled branches, or simply among dense foliage. These are the same trees that the birds require for nesting, and in which each pair creates its nest that's simply a clutter of sticks and other scraps of wood.

Anyone who has a close encounter with one of these magnificent predators, which might return a human's gaze of wonder with a sleepy blink of its golden eyes, will need little convincing of the need to preserve the habitats of this glorious bird of prey that has the alternative name of 'winking owl', for without it wild Australia would undoubtedly be a poorer place.

Juvenile Barking Owl in the author's garden.

# OTHER NON-PASSERINES

## AUSTRALIAN BUSTARD
*Ardeotis australis*

With flocks of several hundred bustards strolling across the grasslands of Australia, early European pioneers had a source of food right on their doorstep, and they enthusiastically hunted the large birds that they knew as 'plains turkeys.' Their insatiable appetite for this meaty bush tucker saw populations of bustards rapidly diminish as settlers colonised new areas and brought sheep and cattle to graze on the grasslands that the birds inhabited. Fortunately, the bustard has survived the onslaught, and these large birds, although in greatly reduced numbers, can still be found in inland and northern areas of the continent, where they're usually seen alone, in pairs or in small groups.

The bustard, with its predominantly grey to brown plumage, is one of Australia's largest birds. Its back and wings are coffee coloured and speckled with dark brown, it has a relatively short brown tail, a long light brown to grey neck, a similarly coloured head with a black crown, a white eyebrow above each of its golden-yellow eyes, cream to white underparts and a grey bill.

These nomadic birds, with their

Australian Bustard on the plains of western Queensland.

Australian Bustard near Tambo, western Queensland.

wanderlust triggered solely by the necessity to find food and water, spend much of their time on the ground where they walk along slowly in an arrogant pose with the neck held erect and the head sloping backwards. They prowl slowly through grasses and low vegetation in search of the wide range of foods that include grasshoppers and other insects, small reptiles, rodents, frogs, foliage, fruit and seeds.

If disturbed, they simply stand still as though a lack of motion provides invisibility, or merely stroll away from any perceived threat while appearing to display little concern about what's going on in the vicinity. Taking to the skies is always a last resort, and although bustards often roost in a tree, they'll frequently settle down to sleep on the ground of the treeless plains that are a dominant feature of their habitat.

Males strut their stuff more energetically and put on an entertaining performance when they're eager to attract a mate, and each strides backwards and forwards, with its tail raised, while emitting a loud roaring noise that's produced by the bird's inflated throat-sac. The female lays one or two large eggs, either on the bare ground or on some grass, where her survival and that of the chicks that will ultimately hatch is in the hands of fate.

People no longer relish the taste of roast bustard but other predators, including foxes, feral cats and dingoes, have no qualms about feasting on the eggs and the vulnerable chicks of this great bird of the plains.

Emus in outback South Australia.

# EMU
*Dromaius novaehollandiae*

In 1696, when a Dutch ship sailed past the coast of Western Australia in search of survivors from a shipwreck, its captain, Willem de Vlamingh, recorded an amazing sight. He saw a gigantic bird that was later identified as the 'New Holland Cassowary.' It's known today as the Emu, an iconic species that has pride of place on the Australian coat of arms.

The name 'Emu' is thought to have originated from an Arabic word meaning 'a big bird', and with a height of around 2m it is the largest bird in Australia and the second largest in the world after the African Ostrich.

Emus thrived in Tasmania until 1865 when the last surviving bird vanished into the shadows of history, but large numbers of these majestic birds still thrive on the mainland where they can be seen dawdling along on their own, in small groups,

Emus near Wanaaring, outback New South Wales.

Emus in outback South Australia.

or in immense flocks.

Although they're often regarded as residents of arid and semi-arid inland regions, they also frequent coastal and hinterland areas, and are occasionally seen wandering along sandy beaches, strolling across golf courses and meandering through agricultural crops. In such situations they're rarely welcome. Only dense forests and the most barren of deserts are excluded from the Emu's range, and although these great flightless birds usually steer clear of urban areas, severe droughts force them to venture into outback settlements in a desperate search for food and water.

*Dromaius*, the name of the genus to which the Emu belongs, is derived from a Greek word meaning 'racer', and although it cannot fly, the Emu can race along the ground, with its long neck outstretched and its thick skirt of feathers billowing in the wind, at a speed in excess of 40km/h.

The long shaggy feathers that cover its body can be in varying shades of brown or grey, with birds that inhabit cool and damp areas having darker plumage than those that

Emu chicks at Currawinya National Park, outback Queensland.

live in warmer and drier climates. The Emu's neck has only a light covering of feathers, with some areas having nothing more than bare blue skin. It has amber-coloured eyes with translucent secondary eyelids that move horizontally across the eyes to provide protection from dust, and with huge claws on its huge feet, the Emu has the perfect weapons with which to fight off any of its own species that are unwelcome in its territory.

Emus are far from particular about what they eat, and although the main ingredients of their diet are grasses, the fruits and flowers of native plants, and other vegetation, including the foliage of acacias and casuarinas, they'll also feast on spiders and a range of insects and their larvae. They regularly ingest small stones too, for these are an essential aid to their digestive system, and they wash it all down with copious amounts of water.

Emus communicate via a series of booming and grunting sounds. The male does most of the grunting, primarily during the breeding season, but also when his mate

Emus in outback South Australia.

is laying her eggs and to alert other males to the fact that they're not welcome in his domain. It's the female who does most of the booming, a sound that's created in her inflatable throat pouch, and that's part of a courtship display as well as a warning to other birds that may be tempted to encroach on her territory.

The breeding behaviour of the Emu is unusual to say the least. After fighting to claim the most desirable male, the female lays a clutch of up to 15 large dark green eggs in a simple nest on the ground, and walks away to leave the male to get on with the demanding task of raising a family as a single parent. Even hunger and thirst fail to lure him away from his paternal duty, and although he occasionally moves momentarily to turn the eggs, he neither eats nor drinks during the eight weeks that he patiently incubates the eggs, and by the time the chicks, cloaked in pyjamas of striped and fluffy down, emerge from the eggs, old man Emu has lost a third of his body weight. He's the most dedicated of fathers, and it's he alone who tends to the young birds that he aggressively defends from predators and from other Emus until, as the next breeding season approaches, his offspring are ready to claim their own place in the world.

Each female, providing she can find a mate who isn't too preoccupied with his parental duties, can lay several clutches of

Male Emu with chicks drinking from the Paroo River at Currawinya National Park, outback Queensland.

eggs each year, and predators enjoy nothing more than a nutritious meal of Emu eggs or succulent chicks.

Some people regard the Emu more as a curse than as an iconic national treasure, with farmers being among the first to complain when the birds' populations soar, and in 1932 landowners were at their most vociferous. Wheat farmers in the Campion region of Western Australian saw their livelihoods under threat when an army of approximately 20,000 Emus arrived on their doorstep, and having found ample supplies of food and water, the invading hordes brazenly staked their claim to ownership of the land. The government instigated a management strategy that became known as The Great Emu War, but the military operation to cull the birds using machine guns began as a farce with only a few birds initially killed. Eventually around 1,000 were shot, and with the threat barely reduced, farmers continued to demand assistance, but their requests were denied. Finally a bounty system was initiated, and with a price on their heads, more than 57,000 Emus were killed in a six-month period during 1934.

Despite the slaughter the birds still thrive in huge numbers, thanks to the increased availability of water sources that have been provided for livestock in semi-arid areas. With Emus now farmed for their meat, oil, feathers and hides, these imposing birds look set to saunter across the Australian landscape for centuries to come.

Laughing Kookaburra in the author's garden.

# LAUGHING KOOKABURRA

*Dacelo novaeguineae*

The Laughing Kookaburra owes its name to the Aboriginal word *guuguubarra*, and it's the bird's early morning call that has led to its alternative name of 'laughing jackass.' This familiar sound of the bush, according to an Aboriginal legend, reminds the mythical people of the sky that it's time to light the fires of the sun to illuminate and warm the earth. Studies of the varied calls of this iconic bird have revealed that each has a specific meaning, with some proclaiming the bird's territory, while others alert its mates to danger, let them know that there's food on offer, or announce that someone's on the lookout for a mate.

Kookaburras make themselves at home in woodlands and open forests in the eastern, south-eastern, and south-western regions of the continent, and have been introduced into Tasmania. In the latter part of the 19th century they were introduced to New Zealand, but only those that were released on Kawau Island survived.

The Laughing Kookaburra is a stocky bird with a predominantly dark brown back, and wings that are of a similar colour with flecks of light blue. The plumage of its head, neck, throat and underparts is a creamy-white flecked with light brown, and it has a short broad tail that's cream with dark brown horizontal stripes, a grey bill and a narrow chocolate-brown streak from each of its dark eyes to the back of its neck.

Kookaburras, despite being members of the kingfisher family, seem to find the concept of catching fish about as appealing as most of us would find a weekend in a broom cupboard, and although they'll dive into a garden pond to catch a goldfish that's easy prey, fish are generally not high on their menu. Sitting silently and motionlessly on a fence post or the branch of a tree, they often appear as energetic as comatose barnacles, but they're not couch potatoes, simply birds that have an abundance of patience, and they'll watch and wait in silence until an unsuspecting victim wanders across the ground below. They're also avid scroungers that frequent picnic areas with optimism that someone will eventually donate a snack, and they're attracted by the flames of bushfires where a roasted meal may be on offer. Small snakes, lizards, rodents, yabbies, frogs, snails, the small chicks of other birds and insects are all components of their varied menu, and when grasshoppers are in plague proportions they form a major part of the kookaburra's diet.

These monogamous birds, which spend their entire lives with the same mate, are highly sociable characters that, although

Laughing Kookaburra at a caravan park on the Sunshine Coast, Queensland.

Laughing Kookaburra at a camping area in Towarri National Park near Scone, New South Wales.

Laughing Kookaburra in the author's garden.

they're often seen alone, are usually members of a close-knit family group. In the breeding season they nest in a hollow within a tree or in a chamber that they have laboriously carved out in a termites' nest that's on a tree trunk high above the ground, and it's then that the family all pull together. Young birds, which remain with the group for several years, are on the bottom rung of the social ladder and, for the first four years of their lives, they're the dog's bodies of the group, helping to defend the family's territory, assisting in the tedious role of incubating the dominant female's eggs, and fetching food for successive generations of chicks and fledglings. During this phase of their lives they don't breed, which means that the reproduction rate of kookaburras is relatively low, but with the dedicated care and attention of all members of their family, the one or two chicks that emerge from each nest have a high chance of survival, and with individual birds having a life expectancy of up to 12 years, these iconic and appealing members of the bushland community are certainly not knocking on the door of extinction.

Australian Brush-turkey on the beach at a camping area near Rainbow Beach, Queensland.

# AUSTRALIAN BRUSH-TURKEY

*Alectura lathami*

The brush-turkey is the largest and most common of Australia's three megapodes, a group of birds that construct huge nesting mounds and that also includes the Orange-footed Scrubfowl and the Malleefowl.

The brush-turkey's range extends through eastern Australia, from Cape York Peninsula in northern Queensland to central New South Wales, and although it inhabits rainforests and damp eucalypt forests and woodlands, it can also be found in drier bushland environments.

It's a large and distinctive bird with a black back, wings, and upper chest, mottled grey and white underparts, a large black tail that fans out vertically, light brown eyes and a black bill. With its vivid red head and neck that's devoid of all but a few spiky feathers, and a bright yellow throat-wattle that during the breeding season becomes larger in males, the brush-turkey, even in the darkest shadows of a forest, stands out like an emu in a hen house.

Male on his nesting mound at Keppel Sands, central Queensland.

Brush-turkey in the author's garden.

These are birds that are easy to please when it comes to food, and as they energetically scratch among the leaf litter and other natural debris that carpets the ground, they'll gobble down almost anything that they find, including insects, worms, centipedes, fallen fruits and seeds. They do an excellent job of controlling insect pests, but no one's happy to see a male brush-turkey rampaging through their garden as he gathers material for his immense nesting mound. He'll tenaciously scratch up everything in what he sees as his kingdom, and any attempt to deter him from wreaking havoc is almost doomed to failure, for he'll simply flutter to safety and resume his task once the coast is clear again, and will eventually create a nesting mound that can be 4m in diameter and 1m high. He renovates the mound every year, simply by adding more scavenged material, and once he's

satisfied with his accomplishment, he heads off in search of a mate.

Several females lay their eggs in the same mound that, in a single breeding season, may contain around 20 eggs that have been carefully covered with a thick layer of plant material. With their eggs safely tucked away, the females return to the bush to resume their lives with no concern for their future offspring. The eggs are incubated solely by the heat generated by the decomposition of the vegetation of the nesting mound, and the male regularly checks the temperature within the mound by digging small holes in it and testing it with a highly sensitive area near his bill. He then adds or removes material as required to regulate the temperature.

The eggs make a tasty meal for predators such as goannas, but if Lady Luck is on their side and the brush-turkey has done his job well, after a seven-week

Brush-turkey chicks are completely independent from the moment they hatch.

incubation period a horde of chicks emerge from the eggs and instinctively dig themselves out of the mound of debris. If they were expecting doting parents to be waiting on the doorstep to provide them with food and protection, they'd be very disappointed, for brush-turkey chicks are on their own from the moment they emerge into the world. Mother Nature is the only parent they'll ever know, and she has endowed the chicks with the abilities they require to survive alone, for they step into the world fully feathered and with the instinctive knowledge of what to eat and where to find it, and within an hour or two

they have also mastered the art of flight.

Even adults are not the most graceful of birds when they take to the air, and they fly only to escape from danger or to roost in trees. They're confident and bold characters that are admired by some people and despised by others, for although they play a valuable role in the wild world, they can be very destructive in an urban environment. Land clearing has destroyed much of their original habitat and their populations have declined since the first Europeans stepped onto Australia's shores, but brush-turkeys are sure to be enthralling and annoying humans for many years to come.

# HONEYEATERS

## BLUE-FACED HONEYEATER

*Entomyzon cyanotis*

With 70 unique species, honeyeaters are the largest family of birds in Australia, and few are more recognisable than the Blue-faced Honeyeater. It's a resident of northern and eastern Australia, with its range also extending from the Kimberley region of Western Australia to southern areas of South Australia. Eucalypt woodlands, melaleuca swamps and mangrove wetlands are among its favoured haunts, and when there's food to be had, the Blue-faced Honeyeater will visit urban parks and gardens too.

It's one of Australia's largest honeyeaters and, with a patch of vivid blue skin around each of its pale yellow eyes it's also one of the most distinctive. Adults have a black head, face and neck, a white streak across the back of the neck, and a dark grey throat and upper breast, while the upper parts of their bodies and wings are olive-green, and their underparts are white. The plumage of juveniles is almost identical to that of their

Feeding on callistemon flowers at Gladstone, Queensland.

Blue-faced Honeyeater at an outdoor café near Gin Gin, Queensland.

Juvenile Blue-faced Honeyeaters have a greenish face.

The search for sweet treats often brings Blue-faced Honeyeaters into parks and gardens.

parents, but they have one feature that sets them apart, for their facial skin, rather than being blue, is bright yellow or lime-green.

The natural diet of these beautiful birds includes nectar and fruit from a wide range of native and exotic plants, and with their penchant for snacking on the flowers and fruit of banana trees, they're often known as 'banana birds'. Although insects form a major part of their diet, it's the Blue-faced Honeyeaters' passion for anything sweet that occasionally gets them into trouble, for they'll confidently descend onto the tables of outdoor cafes to peck at any momentarily unattended food, and will even lift the lid of a sugar bowl to feast on its contents.

They demonstrate considerable acrobatic skills and agility in their efforts to reach flowers that are at the tips of fragile stems and will aggressively, and with considerable noise and a burst of frenetic activity, chase most other birds from their feeding area.

When the time comes to lay their eggs, Blue-faced Honeyeaters are not particularly energetic, and although they occasionally construct a cup-shaped nest of bark that they line with grass, they rarely waste any time on such mundane domestic duties. They're happy to commandeer nests that have been abandoned by other birds, and after a quick makeover with a few strips of bark added here and there, the female gives it her approval and settles down to the serious business of laying her eggs.

Blue-faced Honeyeaters are often seen feeding on the nectar of flowers.

Above and opposite: Brown Honeyeater in the author's garden.

## BROWN HONEYEATER

*Lichmera indistincta*

The small and slim Brown Honeyeater is a relatively timid bird that blends quietly into the landscape. With a yellow tinge to its brown wings, brown upper body, creamy-brown underparts and a curved black bill, it's certainly not the most glamorous of birds, with its only dash of colour being a small pale yellow splash of feathers behind each eye, but despite its rather drab appearance, it's a charismatic little character that has a cheerful song, and that's fascinating to watch, whether it's alone, with a mate, or in a small group.

It's a species that's widespread in Australia, and that can be found throughout the mainland, with the exception of south-eastern Australia and arid inland regions. It makes itself at home in a wide range of habitats, including eucalypt woodlands, forests that shadow meandering waterways, damp rainforests, and swathes of mangroves that dip their toes in the mud of river estuaries. In semi-arid regions, providing there's a source of water nearby, this diminutive honeyeater will flutter contentedly among mallee scrub, through woodlands carpeted with spinifex grass, and among the low vegetation surrounding saline marshes. When there's food on offer, the Brown Honeyeater has no hesitation in taking up residence in an urban park or a home garden.

It feeds on nectar and scoffs any small insects that cross its path, and it's an extremely agile and almost hyperactive bird as it forages among the foliage and flowers of trees and shrubs. Although it often shares its habitat with other honeyeaters, its more aggressive neighbours, such as White-throated Honeyeaters and friarbirds, will frequently chase it away from clusters of flowers and from the edge of water, and being a generally non-aggressive neighbour it usually takes the hint and forages or drinks elsewhere.

When it's time to start a family, the male Brown Honeyeater alerts the community to the news with his song, and stands guard while his mate constructs a small cup-shaped nest using melaleuca bark and grass that's held together with cobwebs, but life wasn't meant to be easy for Brown Honeyeaters. Their nests are often commandeered by cuckoos that callously toss out the honeyeater's eggs and replace them with their own, and when the cuckoo's chicks eventually hatch, the unassuming Brown Honeyeaters, in blissful ignorance, raise the impostors as their own.

Noisy Friarbird.

## NOISY FRIARBIRD
*Philemon corniculatus*

The Noisy Friarbird was first described by ornithologist John Latham in 1790, with its species name derived from the Latin word *corniculum*, meaning 'a little horn', a reference to the prominent lump,

known as a casque, that's on the bird's bill.

It's the astounding array of curious calls that gave birth to the bird's common name, but the Noisy Friarbird is also known as the 'leatherhead' and a 'four-o-clock bird', with the latter name relating to one of its calls that sounds as though it's declaring the hour at various times of the day.

Noisy Friarbirds are found in eastern and south-eastern Australia, from north-eastern Queensland to north-eastern Victoria, but the cooler climate in southern areas of their range is not always to their liking, and many birds migrate north in autumn and return south as winter comes to an end. Eucalypt woodlands, coastal heathlands and the forests that fringe wetlands and rivers in semi-arid and arid regions are the favoured haunts of Noisy Friarbirds which give their presence away as they engage in vociferous and often aggressive disputes with other birds. Even when they're on their own they're rarely quiet for more than a tiny fragment of the day.

With a naked black head, the casque on its black bill and dark red eyes, the Noisy Friarbird is a very distinctive character, but with dull greyish-brown wings and back, and creamy-white plumage on its neck and under its body, it's certainly not the most colourful of birds.

They're far from welcome in some agricultural areas where they satisfy their appetites for the sweet treats of life by feeding on fruit, but although some farmers may see them as the enemy, these large honeyeaters are not always the villains of the story. Their varied diet, in addition to fruit and nectar, includes insects, and being particularly partial to a feast of grasshoppers, they're the invaluable allies of farmers and gardeners in the ongoing battle to control insect pests.

Feeding on callistemon flowers.

At a bird bath.

Noisy Friarbird gathering bark for the construction of its nest. All images taken in the author's garden.

They spend much of their time feeding on the nectar-laden flowers of trees, with the colourful blooms of grevilleas being among their favourites. They demonstrate great agility, put on entertaining acrobatic performances, and find themselves in contorted poses as they reach for flowers at the tips of slender stems that bow beneath their meagre weight.

Noisy Friarbirds stake their claim to a source of food with an astounding array of curious sounds, and chatter on incessantly as though indulging in a lengthy conversation, the main statement of which is undoubtedly 'This is MY tree'. With intense aggression, they chase away other birds, including those of their own species that have the temerity to consider that there might be enough nectar for all to share, but when food is involved, Noisy Friarbirds rarely have any concept of sharing.

They form long-term mating pairs, and as the breeding season approaches, they rip long strips of bark from the trunks of melaleuca trees, for this is the basic material with which they construct their cup-shaped nests. The bark, together with grass, is bound with sticky strands of cobweb, and when the eggs are finally laid in the nest that's well camouflaged among the thick foliage of trees, the bush becomes a quieter place as the Noisy Friarbirds, for a brief period of time, have very little to say.

Male Scarlet Honeyeater. All images taken in the author's garden.

## SCARLET HONEYEATER
*Myzomela sanguinolenta*

The Scarlet Honeyeater is a bird that once seen is never forgotten, and anyone who fails to be awestruck by a glimpse of this small but spectacular creature would have to be as emotive as an inebriated weevil.

Being one of Australia's smallest honeyeaters, and the fact that it spends much of its time foraging for food in the foliage of tall trees, are two good reasons why the Scarlet Honeyeater is not always easily seen, but its musical song provides a clue that it's in the vicinity.

Its range extends from Cooktown in northern Queensland to the Gippsland area of Victoria, but when the icy winds of winter begin to whip across the landscape, the Scarlet Honeyeater abandons the southern section of its range and heads north, where it makes itself at home in coastal and hinterland forests and woodlands.

It's the male that makes the greatest impression on anyone fortunate enough to see him darting through the vegetation,

Female Scarlet Honeyeater.

and with his vivid red head, black back, dark wings and red chest that blurs into the light brown plumage of his underparts, he's a very handsome character indeed. Females are far less colourful, with their dull brown plumage enhanced by little more than a dusting of red across the throat.

The Scarlet Honeyeater's relatively long curved bill is the perfect tool for accessing the nectar hidden within the flowers of native trees, including melaleucas and eucalyptus, and although nectar is the main focus of its feeding activities, it also dines on small fruits and insects.

This diminutive bird prefers to forage, either alone or with a mate, in the upper levels of the forest canopy where it flutters quietly among flowers and foliage, but life isn't always harmonious in the treetops, for these brightly coloured birds attract the attention of the neighbourhood bullies and are frequently attacked by larger and more aggressive honeyeaters with whom they compete for often limited sources of food.

The Scarlet Honeyeater's small cup-shaped nest, made from bark and grass stitched together with cobwebs, can be the nursery for up to three broods of chicks in a single season, and that means that, with the species being far from rare, anyone who's in the right place at the right time will be treated to a glimpse of one of Australia's most dazzling wild residents.

These honeyeaters are among our most brightly coloured birds.

# NOISY MINER
*Manorina melanocephala*

The Noisy Miner's common name is most appropriate, for this is a bird that's rarely quiet for more than the fleeting moment that passes as it flutters from one branch to another. These predominantly grey birds are also known as 'happy family birds', but when in a group their repetitive and rowdy disputes shatter any concept of social harmony.

It's one of the most common honeyeaters in eastern Australia, and inhabits open woodlands in an area that stretches from northern Queensland to Tasmania and west to south-eastern South Australia.

With mottled dark grey to brown plumage on its back and wings, a neck and underparts that are a lighter grey fading to white towards the tail, and dark grey feathers on its crown and cheeks the Noisy Miner wins no prize for glamour. Mother Nature has added some bling to brighten its attire, and with a vivid yellow bill, yellow legs and an equally bright yellow patch of bare skin behind each eye, this relatively small bird is unmistakable.

These are aggressive birds that come together as a raucous mob to attack any predators that offer even a veiled threat. If other birds inadvertently intrude into their territory they have no hesitation, either as a group or as individuals, in launching a

This series of images was taken at Bundaberg Botanic Gardens, Queensland.

These honeyeaters are aggressive to other species.

Noisy Miner on the flowers of a grevillea.

vigorous and unprovoked attack and will frequently chase away much larger birds, including birds of prey. The message is soon passed around, and the domineering attitude of Noisy Miners ensures that other birds steer well clear of areas that are inhabited by a far from welcoming group of these aggressive honeyeaters.

In keeping with their highly social nature, they usually feed in groups rather than on their own. The nectar-rich flowers of grevilleas are among their preferred food sources, and with the birds having become well adapted to urban life, they're regular visitors to parks and gardens when trees and shrubs are blooming.

Noisy Miners are bold and cheeky characters, and will snatch a meal of bread or jam from an outdoor table, but like many honeyeaters they'll also devour insects, particularly when there's a limited supply of fruit and flowers.

They breed in colonies, and while it's the female who constructs the nest from twigs, grass and leaves, and then lays and incubates the eggs, it's during the breeding season that the birds finally begin to work together as a cohesive family unit. Several of the males within the group share the essential chore of feeding the chicks, thus ensuring that the young birds have an optimum chance of survival, and with more than one brood frequently reared during a single season, it's one time when the name 'happy family bird' seems quite appropriate.

White-throated Honeyeater feeding on callistemon flowers.

## WHITE-THROATED HONEYEATER

*Melithreptus albogularis*

White-throated Honeyeaters inhabit a coastal strip that stretches from the Kimberley region of Western Australia, into the Northern Territory, and down the eastern side of the continent as far as northern New South Wales. They live in open woodlands and forests, particularly those close to permanent sources of water, and will happily take up residence in parks and gardens if water and an adequate supply of food are available.

The White-throated Honeyeater has white plumage from the throat down to the underside of the tail. Its back is olive-green to brown, its wings are slightly darker, and its head and neck are as black as ebony.

Collecting nest material from a melaleuca tree.

This series of images was taken in the author's garden.

A narrow band of white feathers wraps around the nape, and there are small white patches of skin above the bird's eyes.

They're usually seen in small flocks, but they can be argumentative among their group and aggressive towards birds of other species that come too close to a source of water or food that the White-throated Honeyeaters are reluctant to share with anyone.

Nectar is high on their list of favoured foods, followed by fruit, insects and spiders, and when it's time for a snack they put on an entertaining performance as, with amazing agility, they clamber among foliage and flowers, often hanging upside-down from fragile stems to reach almost inaccessible blooms.

They have a passion for water, and not merely to quench their thirst, for they love to bathe, and on chilly winter days and in searing summer weather they'll enthusiastically and repetitively dive into the water of a pool or garden bird bath until their feathers become saturated. In such situations they're at the top of the pecking order, with other birds having to wait their turn until the White-throated Honeyeaters retreat to a nearby shrub or tree to preen their feathers and ensure that they look as glamorous as ever.

When they're ready to breed, they construct a cup-shaped nest of bark that's woven together with strands of cobweb, and settle down to produce the next generation of what must be the cleanest birds of wild Australia.

# OTHER PASSERINES

**P**asserines – also known as 'perching birds' – are a group of birds that are distinguished by the arrangement of their toes, with three pointing forward and one back, and that have tendons in their legs that tighten when the leg bends, causing the foot to curl and clamp onto a perch so that the bird can sleep without falling off.

## WHITE-WINGED CHOUGH
*Corcorax melanorhamphus*

**T**he White-winged Chough, a resident of the forests and woodlands of eastern and south-eastern Australia, with the exception of northern Queensland, might not be the most glamorous of birds, but when it comes to personality it's an unrivalled star.

White wing-patches, which are usually only visible during flight, are the obvious reason for its common name, but with the

During a summer heatwave White-winged Choughs appreciated the cool water of a fountain.

On a summer's day White-winged Choughs cool off in a bird bath.

rest of its plumage being black this is a bird that's often mistaken for a crow, but its bright red eyes and curved dark grey to black bill set it apart from other equally black species.

White-winged Choughs are not particularly elegant when in flight, for they flutter around with a slow flapping action that's interspersed with short bursts of gliding, but their lack of skill in the air is of no concern to these highly sociable birds, for they spend the majority of the day on the ground.

In chattering family groups of up to 15 birds they stroll confidently across grasslands, woodlands, agricultural areas, and urban parks and gardens. With their complex vocabulary of sounds they continually communicate with one another as they rummage among fallen leaves, and feast on worms and snails, insects including ants, bees and wasps, and a wide range of seeds and small fruits. One distinctive call brings other members of the group running to share the delicacies that have been unearthed, while another message sounds the alarm when there's a hint of danger. In such a situation the birds initially do nothing more than run, but if a threat persists, they fly up, squawking loudly, into the low branches of nearby trees until it's safe to resume their leisurely terrestrial way of life.

When the breeding season arrives, every member of the group, which usually consists of a breeding pair and their offspring, dutifully assists in the construction of a large bowl-shaped nest that's made with mud

White-winged Choughs in the author's garden.

reinforced with fragments of bark and other plant material and located on a high branch. Every bird also helps to incubate the eggs, to feed the chicks, and to defend the nest and its tiny occupants from predators.

When the fledglings finally take the courageous decision to leave the nest, their first adventure is merely a brief and fluttering flight to the ground. They scamper along after other members of the group, quickly learning the ropes, noisily begging for food from older birds, and instinctively realising that survival depends on a rapid response to the alarm calls of the family.

Young birds take four years to reach maturity, and during this time they remain with their parents, and in the logic of White-winged Choughs, the more the merrier is the key to survival. An increased number of birds within the group means that there's a greater chance of spotting predators while there's still time to escape, and occasionally, to maximise the population of their group, White-winged Choughs turn to a little villainy and kidnap the chicks of neighbouring families.

Above and opposite: Double-barred Finch in the author's garden.

## DOUBLE-BARRED FINCH

*Taeniopygia bichenovii*

In the early half of the 19th century, James Ebenezer Bicheno, the colonial secretary of Van Diemen's Land, who was also a botanist and a farmer, proclaimed that "gardening advances civilisation by combining the innocent, useful and beautiful," and he was spot on with that observation. He might never have considered that his name would be immortalised in connection with anything other than a memorable quote, but he was mistaken, for his name is now tied to one of Australia's smallest and most charismatic birds that goes by the far from easy to pronounce scientific name of *Taeniopygia bichenovii*.

It's a species that's at home in the northern and eastern regions of the continent, and in inland areas where there are woodlands and bushland with an understorey of grasses.

A white face surrounded with a black band has earned it the colloquial name of 'owl-faced finch', and it's the second black band across its white chest that has led to it being christened with the more familiar name of 'Double-barred Finch'.

It's not a bird endowed with plumage in dazzling and gaudy hues, for its head and back are merely light brown, its wings are black with white spots, its relatively long tail is black and its bill and legs are a drab shade of grey. While it might not be the most glamorous character on the block, the entertaining and energetic activities of this

diminutive bird make it a delight to watch as it goes about its daily life with incessant and cheerful chirping.

Double-barred Finches, which often flutter across the landscape in flocks of 40–50 birds, are primarily seed-eaters, and are most at home in environments where grasses provide an ample supply of seeds and low shrubs offer shelter and nesting sites. They generally feed on the ground, and will dine on insects in addition to seeds, particularly when they have hungry chicks to satisfy.

These are birds that are passionate about building nests, although their techniques are relatively primitive and the resultant construction is certainly no avian mansion. A pair will spend many hours every day flying back and forth to and from their nesting site, which is usually in a tree or a shrub with dense foliage. The materials they utilise frequently far exceed the length of the bird's body, and long stems of grass, fragments of other plant material, and strands of animal or human hair trail behind them as they fly towards the construction site where they laboriously drag each prize through the tangle of leaves. The result of their endeavours is a rather scruffy spherical nest, with an entrance in one side. Several pairs often build their nests in the same tree, but when the task is completed, it's not necessarily breeding that's on the mind of these tiny birds, for many use their nests simply as places to roost during the night or to shelter from inclement weather.

Above and opposite: Grey Shrike-thrush in the author's garden.

# GREY SHRIKE-THRUSH
*Colluricincla harmonica*

**M**any people wouldn't give the drab Grey Shrike-thrush a second glance, but looks can be deceptive, for this is a bird that puts on a spectacular performance as it struts confidently across Mother Nature's outdoor stage. The show goes on, day after day, in woodlands, parks and urban gardens in all but the most arid regions.

Its highly variable plumage ranges from primarily grey in the eastern areas of its range to predominantly brown in the north, while birds in western areas have a combination of both colours. While there's no argument about the fact that the Grey Shrike-thrush's attire is far from outstanding, when it performs its staggering repertoire of melodious songs, no one could contest the claim that this is the best songbird in the country.

It sings while it's resting on a perch, when it's admiring its own reflection in the window of a building, and when, on its own or with a mate, it's searching for food. This far from fussy eater rummages among the foliage of trees or on the ground for the ingredients of its varied diet, which include insects, spiders, frogs and small lizards, with the main course occasionally followed by a dessert of small fruits and seeds. For some other birds, the song of the Grey Shrike-thrush is a warning of imminent danger, for this charismatic and seemingly placid bird has a far less pleasant side to its character. It's a predator that's more than eager to feed on the eggs and helpless chicks of its neighbours.

Grey Shrike-thrushes are usually monogamous, and a pair generally inhabits the same extensive territory during their entire lives together. They're creatures of habit, or so it appears, for a pair often constructs their cup-shaped nest in the same spot every year, and both male and female share the tasks of nest-building, incubating the eggs, and feeding the chicks that eventually hatch and that give these cheerful entertainers something else to sing about.

# AUSTRALIAN MAGPIE
*Gymnorhina tibicen*

**T**he Australian Magpie's species name *tibicen* is a Latin word meaning 'flute player,' and while this most familiar of birds lacks the ability to play any musical instrument, it has a wide array of delightful and melodious calls.

Adult male magpie in parklands in Gin Gin, Queensland.

It's a distinctive bird that's readily recognised by almost every Australian, for it can be seen wherever there's a combination of both trees and open areas, and that means that the magpie is equally at home in cities and towns as it is in woodlands and agricultural areas. Only the densest of forests and the most barren deserts are devoid of these charismatic characters.

The pattern of the magpie's plumage varies slightly across its range, but in most areas the majority of its body is black, with males generally having white feathers on the nape, the edges of the wings, and the upper section of the tail. In females, these areas are usually light grey, and although juveniles wear similar attire to that of their parents, they have mottled grey feathers on their underparts and on their backs.

Magpies have a varied diet that includes worms, small lizards, insects, spiders, mice and frogs. If times are tough, they'll stoop to eating seeds and fruit, and will occasionally dine on the most unpalatable of prey – the introduced and poisonous Cane Toad. They've discovered that, by flipping one of these repulsive creatures over onto its back, they can eat its soft belly – which is devoid of the harmful toxins that the toad exudes from other parts of its skin – and live to tell the tale.

When they're hunting for more elusive prey, magpies, with their highly sensitive hearing, dawdle along the ground listening for the sounds of insects and their larvae that might be wriggling in the soil beneath their feet. When they're confident that there's life within their reach, they stab the soil with their pointed bills and pull out their doomed and struggling prey.

Magpies are also opportunists that will grab a free snack wherever it's on offer. They gatecrash barbecues and picnics, waiting patiently on the sidelines for whatever scraps are tossed their way or left behind by human diners. They loiter close to campfires and bushfires for any roasted treats that may be available once the fury of the flames has died. They arrive uninvited on the doorsteps of houses where residents are happy to feed them in return for nothing more than the pleasure of sharing a moment of their lives in the company of these wild creatures, and perhaps being rewarded with a song.

The magpie's voice is one of the iconic sounds of the Australian bush and of the corners of suburbia that it also inhabits, and while these appealing birds can mimic the calls of many other species, it's the magpie's own unique song that has earned it a place in the hearts of many Australians. The renowned 19th century British ornithologist, artist and writer John Gould commented that: "to describe the note of this bird is beyond the power of my pen," but other authors have attempted to write the words to the magpie's most common song, and in one wag's opinion it sounds

Juvenile Australian Magpie.

like: "Waddle, giggle, gargle" and "quardle, oodle, ardle, wardle, doodle."

Magpies, which can reach the ripe old age of 25 years, live in small and highly territorial groups, and although they generally interact peacefully with humans, they can become extremely aggressive during the breeding season. A group may contain several females that are all intent on raising a family, but the duties of fatherhood are usually all down to one male who has a hectic time mating with all the females and defending the group's extensive territory. People who venture too close to a nesting site are seen as a threat and come under attack from swooping male magpies, and it's then that these birds, which are loved by so many, become the subject of fear and hatred.

There was no hint of fear, only of amazement, among a group of scientists who, when recently investigating the movements and social behaviour of magpies, made an amazing discovery that sheds new light on

Eastern Yellow Robin eating hairy caterpillar at a camping area beside the Mann River, northern New South Wales.

the lives of these most familiar of birds. The researchers attached tiny tracking devices with backpack-like harnesses to five magpies. Just 10 minutes after the final tracker had been fitted an adult female magpie, who had already removed her tracker, began working to remove the harness from a younger bird. The group worked together to free themselves of the devices, and by the third day they had removed the last one. Such a seemingly altruistic act revealed a previously unknown facet of the behaviour of these intelligent and highly sociable birds – for they assisted other members of their group simply because it was the right thing to do.

## EASTERN YELLOW ROBIN
### *Eopsaltria australis*

*Eopsaltria*, the name of the genus to which this colourful robin belongs, is an ancient word that means 'singer of the dawn,' and it's an appropriate description, for in the forests and woodlands that it inhabits, the Eastern Yellow Robin is invariably the first bird to welcome each new day. It begins its repetitive and monotonous song, a series of five or six high-pitched beeps, often well before the sun has tossed its first rays of light across the horizon, and it's impossible to ignore

Mother Nature's most reliable alarm clock.

This attractive little robin is a resident of eastern mainland Australia, with its range including coastal and adjacent hinterland areas from northern Queensland to the eastern section of South Australia. It brings a vibrant dash of colour to the shadows of eucalypt woodlands and rainforests, mallee and acacia scrub, and coastal heathlands as alone, with a mate or as a member of a small family group, it flutters through the vegetation. Urban parks and gardens that include suitable habitats will also tempt Eastern Yellow Robins to make themselves at home.

Both sexes are of a similar appearance, with a grey back and head, grey wings with black tips, a light grey throat, vivid yellow underparts, a yellow rump and a black bill, but young birds, with plumage that's primarily of a reddish-brown colour, bear little resemblance to their parents and fool many people into assuming that they're members of a completely different species.

Being out and about before many other birds, the Eastern Yellow Robin is definitely the early bird that gets the worm, or at least the juiciest of insects, for it's insects, including moths, grasshoppers, ants, wasps and flies, in addition to spiders, that routinely satisfy its appetite. It discovers food among the foliage of trees, and occasionally catches insects when in flight, but most of its prey are caught on the ground and are victims of the robin's well-honed hunting technique that utilises patience, speed and the element of surprise. In its distinctive pose, the Eastern Yellow Robin clings to the trunk of a tree from where it scans the ground for any hint of a meal. When it spots something that takes its fancy, it pounces onto the doomed creature, scoffs it, and returns to its lookout position to wait for the next course on the menu to meander past.

As the breeding season gets under way, females get in the construction mood and, in the high fork of a tree, they build their small cup-shaped nests from grass and fragments of twigs that are laced together with silken strands of cobweb. Each female may lay up to three clutches of eggs in a single season, and that's a good insurance policy, for parasitic cuckoos frequently destroy the eggs of robins and replace them with their own.

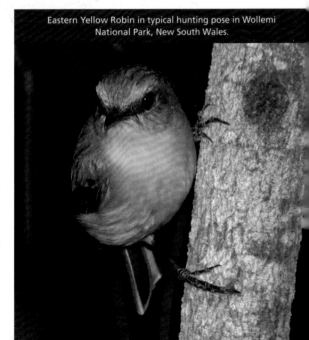

Eastern Yellow Robin in typical hunting pose in Wollemi National Park, New South Wales.

# GOLDEN WHISTLER
*Pachycephala pectoralis*

The male Golden Whistler, with his regal plumage, is the unchallenged king of colour in any forest or woodland that he inhabits in an extensive range that stretches from northern Queensland to south-eastern areas of the mainland and to Tasmania, and that also includes southern regions of Western Australia. Any habitat with a relatively dense covering of trees, from eucalypt woodlands and mallee scrub to rainforests, attracts these glorious birds, and they'll happily take up residence in urban parks and gardens if there are adequate trees to satisfy their demands.

The male is most eye-catching, for he has vivid yellow plumage on the underparts, olive-green to yellow back and wings, black head with a yellow collar, black bill, chestnut-brown eyes and white throat that's separated from his yellow chest by a wide black band. The female, with her dull grey-brown plumage, rarely captures the attention of anyone other than her mate.

Golden Whistlers usually feed alone and forage among the foliage of trees for insects and spiders, with small native fruits also on the menu, but when the breeding season arrives they come together to mate and to share the task of building a nest. The shallow bowl-shaped structure, created with twigs, grass and fragments of bark bound together with cobwebs, is no palace, but the new generation of Golden Whistlers that will be raised within it are guaranteed to bring another touch of majestic beauty to their forest home.

Golden Whistler in the author's garden.

Male at Wallingat National Park, New South Wales.

## SUPERB FAIRY-WREN

*Malurus cyaneus*

In 1777, William Anderson, a naturalist who accompanied Captain James Cook on his third voyage to Australia, brought a specimen of the Superb Fairy-wren on board the creaking ship, and his fellow travellers must have been as blind as a mob of fossilised bed bugs if they remained unimpressed by the beauty of this tiny creature.

Fortunately, there are plenty of opportunities for modern-day Australians to be awestruck by this beautiful bird too, for it's

Male at Wallingat National Park, New South Wales.

Juvenile or non-breeding male at Dorrigo National Park, New South Wales.

found in south-eastern Queensland, New South Wales, Victoria, the south-eastern corner of South Australia and Tasmania, where it inhabits woodlands with dense undergrowth, grasslands with scattered low shrubs, and areas with thickets of introduced plants such as lantana and blackberry. Superb Fairy-wrens are also regular visitors to urban parks and gardens. Never shy to introduce themselves, they'll dart enthusiastically across the landscape and, with their hyperactive antics, will entertain and mesmerise anyone who has the honour of being in their presence.

It's the male that elicits the greatest gasps of delight from those who see him, particularly when wearing his breeding plumage, for it's when he's ready to start a new family that his drab brown feathers are exchanged for ones of a brighter hue. With an iridescent blue forehead and face-patches, swathes of blue across the top of his back, a dark blue tail, a black throat and a brown chest and wings, this tiny bird is indeed superb. Once males reach four years of age they retain their vivid plumage throughout the year, but younger non-breeding males are barely distinguishable from the brown females, except for the fact that their tails are dark blue while those of females are brown, and they lack the orange patch around each eye that is a distinctive feature of the female.

They live in family groups comprising a single female, a dominant male, several non-breeding males and a few juveniles. A male, as part of his courtship display, often presents a female with the yellow petals of a flower, and eventually, among low and dense vegetation, the pair construct a domed nest from grass and cobwebs. When the eggs eventually hatch, all members of the group attend to the chore of feeding the chicks, and when the fledglings take their first hesitant steps into the world beyond the nest, the other birds within the group continue to provide them with food, and with her brood well cared for, the female nests again before the breeding season comes to its conclusion.

Foxes and cats prey on vulnerable chicks, but their future is in jeopardy right from the moment a female lays her eggs, for cuckoos play their age-old trick on these unsuspecting birds. They lay their eggs in the nests of Superb Fairy-wrens and, when the cuckoo's eggs hatch, the chicks condemn the fairy-wren's offspring to a certain death by tossing them out of the nest. Superb Fairy-wrens have become wise to the deception however and, alerted by the unfamiliar begging call of the impostor that has taken their chicks' place, they frequently abandon the nest and leave the baby cuckoo to starve. Evolution has now taken the cuckoos' side however, for these parasitic birds, according to researchers, have begun to imitate the call of a fairy-wren chick, and are thus more likely to be accepted and raised by their foster parents.

Juvenile or non-breeding male at Wollemi National Park, New South Wales.

These confident little birds are easily recognised by their distinctive plumage and erect tails as, with animated hops and bounces, they forage on the ground and among low shrubs for insects that are the major component of their diet. They also dine on seeds, flowers and earthworms, and during winter, when other food may be scarce, they satisfy their hunger with ants. Just like the crew on Captain's Cook's ship, any modern-day birdwatcher is sure to be mesmerised by the undeniable beauty of this most sociable of birds that, in a 2021 poll conducted by *The Guardian* newspaper and Birdlife Australia, narrowly defeating the Tawny Frogmouth for the title of Bird of The Year.

Male at Wallingat National Park, New South Wales.

White-browed Scrubwren in the author's garden.

## WHITE-BROWED SCRUBWREN

*Sericornis frontalis*

At first glance, the White-browed Scrub-wren might be seen as a drab and unappealing character, but this is a bird with a vibrant personality that makes it one of the avian celebrities of the bush. It's the most common of the five species of scrubwrens that call Australia home, and is a resident of the rainforests, woodlands and heaths of a coastal region that stretches from northern Queensland to around Adelaide in South Australia.

Each has a dark brown bill, red legs, dark

White-browed Scrubwren in the author's garden.

grey to brown plumage on its head and back, similarly coloured wings with white streaks on the top section, dark grey to black face, white stripe both above and below each of its pale yellow eyes, white throat and a cream breast, with the rest of its underparts being brown.

White-browed Scrubwrens, which usually live with a mate or in a small family group, spend most of their time on the ground among low and dense vegetation where they feast on insects and enjoy the occasional snack of seeds, but these bold and hyperactive little birds will take food wherever it's on offer and, with minimal hesitation, they'll fly into buildings and even flutter into vehicles if there's a vague hint that a crumb or two might lie unguarded.

They exercise a tad more caution when building a nest however, for each spherical construction is well hidden close to the ground among a tangle of dense vegetation. With all members of the group tending to the needs of the chicks and ensuring that they're well fed and cared for, these endearing little creatures will continue to strut across nature's vast outdoor stage and cast their spell of enchantment over all who see them.

Female Olive-backed Sunbird. These images were taken in Cairns Botanic Gardens, Queensland.

## OLIVE-BACKED SUNBIRD

*Nectarinia jugularis*

This is a bird of the tropics, with its range limited to the north-eastern coastal region of Queensland, from the tip of Cape York south to around Gladstone. Although its natural habit is among the trees and shrubs of wetlands and mangrove swamps, the Olive-backed Sunbird is also a regular visitor to parks and gardens that offer adequate sources of food and water, together with vegetation for roosting and shelter.

When the male comes into view he's impossible to ignore, for with a gleaming swathe of metallic dark blue to purple plumage extending from the chin to the upper breast, and the rest of his under body being bright yellow, he's a stunning creature. His back and wings are a more subdued yellowish-brown, and he has a curved bill that allows him to effortlessly reach the nectar of flowers. The female has a similar appearance in most respects, but lacks the iridescent colouration of her mate, with all her underparts being yellow.

Olive-backed Sunbirds not only feed on the blooms produced by a wide range of native trees and shrubs as well as exotic garden plants, but also feast on insects that they frequently catch in flight, and on spiders that the birds skilfully pluck from their sticky webs.

Each breeding pair creates a nest made of bark, grass and leaves held together with cobwebs. The long and distinctive structure, utilising a complex design with a roofed entrance on one side and a central nesting chamber, is generally suspended from a tree or, when constructed by birds that have taken up residence in an urban area, from an artificial structure, such as the exposed beam of a verandah, the edge of a gutter or even a power line, and these colourful and confident little birds, which display minimal fear of humans, vigorously defend their territory against other birds that they may see as a threat to the survival of their chicks.

Above and opposite: Male Olive-backed Sunbird feeding on flowers.

Eastern Grey Kangaroo joey beside its mother at a state forest camp ground in Queensland.

# ANIMALS

## KANGAROOS AND OTHER MACROPODS

**K**angaroos and wallabies are among the approximately 73 species of Australian marsupials that are known collectively as macropods, a term derived from a Greek word meaning 'large-footed.'

The kangaroo features prominently on the Australian coat of arms, and its inclusion is said to be a symbolic reminder that the nation will always move forward and never backwards, for the kangaroo, thanks to its unique anatomy, cannot walk backwards.

Some species of macropods thrive in large numbers and, during the best of seasons, they breed up to a level where their populations are in almost plague proportions, but others, primarily as a result of the destruction of their habitat, have seen their numbers dramatically reduced, with some species teetering on the brink of extinction. It's a situation that John Gould, the acclaimed 19th century English naturalist and artist, warned Australians about in his monumental work *The Mammals of Australia*.

"Short-sighted indeed are the Anglo-Australians, or they would ere this have made laws for the preservation of their highly singular, and in many instances noble, indigenous animals," he wrote. "Let me urge them to bestir themselves, ere it be too late, to establish laws for the preservation of the large kangaroos, the emu and other conspicuous animals; without some such protection, the remnant that is left will soon disappear," he added prophetically. Sadly his words went unheeded for many years.

Red-necked Wallaby joey peering from its mother's pouch at Coolah Tops National Park, New South Wales.

Eastern Grey Kangaroo female and joey.

# EASTERN GREY KANGAROO
*Macropus giganteus*

In Tasmania, where the Eastern Grey is known as the Forester Kangaroo, it's seldom seen anywhere other than in the central and north-eastern regions of the island state, but it's a dramatically different situation on the mainland where it's sometimes regarded as a pest. With more than 16 million bounding across the continent's varied landscapes, seeing one or more of these beautiful creatures is as easy as spotting a glint of gold in the nation's mint.

Eastern Grey Kangaroos thrive on the vast inland plains, but they're also residents of the woodlands, forests and mallee scrub of eastern Australia, and are equally at home in subalpine regions. They have no hesitation whatsoever in settling in urban environments too, particularly during times of drought when they discover that reliable sources of food and water are on offer, but few people throw a welcome party when

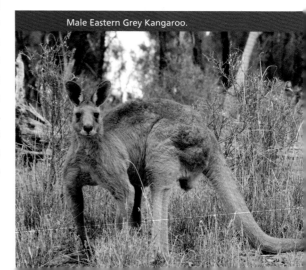
Male Eastern Grey Kangaroo.

these iconic animals adopt golf courses, parklands and gardens as part of their home range, and add the foliage and flowers of ornamental plants to their diet.

When large mobs silently emerge from the remnant native vegetation that's dotted across many agricultural areas, farmers declare war as the roos gorge themselves on valuable crops. In Canberra, the home of the nation's parliament, the battle rages on, for the extensive bushland reserves that are scattered throughout the city are ruled by more than 30,000 Eastern Greys. With an estimated 150–300 animals per square kilometre, they're the Australian Capital Territory's most prominent wild residents, and they demonstrate that, at least for kangaroos, life was definitively meant to be easy as they laze on the verdant lawns of homes that they're eager to share, including the residence of the Governor General.

Although grass forms the major part of their diet, they're highly adaptable creatures that will nibble on a wide range of other vegetation. They'll occasionally eat fungi, and have been recorded feeding on seaweed on coastal beaches. It's that adaptability that has enabled them to survive prolonged periods of drought.

Eastern Greys are very gregarious, and although it's often just mum, dad and a joey hanging out together, with the latest addition to the family occasionally taking a peek at the outside world from the security of its

In northern New South Wales, a large joey Eastern Grey Kangaroo doesn't stray far from its mother's pouch.

mother's pouch, they frequently congregate in large mobs.

They communicate with one another via gentle clucking sounds, throaty growls and harsh coughing noises, and are most active from dusk to dawn. During the day, they adopt a life of relative leisure and rest in the shade, and as summer temperatures soar they lick their forearms and hold them out in a fleeting breeze to reduce their body temperature. Also, like a cat, these meticulously clean animals wash their faces and whiskers by wiping them repetitively with their dampened forearms.

If danger comes their way they're instantly alert and, able to hop across the landscape at speeds up to 60km/h, they make a hasty retreat. In some situations they do the unexpected, for they're not afraid of water and can swim quite efficiently over short distances. The most amazing fact however, is that when a female emerges from the water, after swimming across a river or a lake, her joey, having travelled in its mother's submerged pouch, remains completely dry and is as unaffected by the aquatic experience as by a journey across the arid outback plains.

Eastern Grey Kangaroo, northern New South Wales.

Eastern Grey Kangaroo joey peering from its mother's pouch, northern New South Wales.

Young male Western Grey Kangaroos sparring in Mungo National Park in outback New South Wales.

## WESTERN GREY KANGAROO
*Macropus fuliginosus*

While the colour of their fur is one of the most conspicuous differences between Western and Eastern Greys, it's the shorter gestation period of females of the western species that sets them apart from their eastern relatives, and although they frequently live almost side-by-side, the two species don't interbreed in the wild.

The woodlands and forests of coastal regions of South Australia and western Victoria, together with southern areas of Western Australia, western New South Wales and the vast semi-arid plains of south-western Queensland, are all part of the extensive range of Western Greys.

They are primarily creatures of the night that spend their days taking it easy in a shaded retreat before heading out to feed as the heat of the day dissipates and night begins to draw its ebony curtain across the sky. Although grasses are the primary

Above and opposite: Western Grey Kangaroos in Innes National Park, South Australia.

ingredient of their diet, they'll also feed on the foliage of a wide selection of the shrubs and low trees that thrive within their varied habitats.

They often congregate in relatively large groups, and with the accessibility of watering points for livestock having improved their chances of survival in arid areas, Western Grey Kangaroos, although their numbers fluctuate with good and bad seasons, are thriving. Despite the fact that their population is considerably less than that of some other species of kangaroos, more than 2.3 million of these endearing animals remain part of Australia's spectacular and diverse wildlife community.

Above and opposite: Red-necked Wallaby at Wollemi National Park, New South Wales.

## RED-NECKED WALLABY

*Macropus rufogriseus*

In 1981, archaeologists who were digging in a cavern beside Tasmania's Franklin River made a discovery that sent them into a frenzy of excitement, for they unearthed incontrovertible evidence that this had been the home of a hardy group of humans at the end of the last Ice Age. The cave contained huge quantities of the bones of animals that early Australians had hunted for food, and some 75 per cent of the remains were of Red-necked Wallabies, which in Tasmania are known as Bennett's Wallabies.

The Red-necked Wallaby still thrives on the island that it's called home for millennia, and this most abundant of all wallabies is also a resident of eastern areas of the Australian mainland, where its range stretches from central Queensland to the South Australia and Victoria border region. Its varied habitats include woodlands, both wet and dry forests with an undergrowth of low vegetation, and grasslands that are in close proximity to trees.

With the largest males being around 1.5m in length, and females considerably smaller, the Red-necked Wallaby is less conspicuous than its more imposing relatives, the kangaroos, but while Mother Nature created an animal that's relatively small in stature, she blessed the Red-necked Wallaby with staggeringly good looks. Reddish-brown to grey fur covers most of its upper body. Its underparts are merely pale grey to brown, but with its chestnut-brown neck, shoulders, and head, a dark strip running down the centre of its face, creamy-white cheek-stripes, a black nose and black paws, it's one of the most beautiful of Australia's many wild residents.

In many situations it's a solitary animal that shares its life with a mate only during the breeding season, but when there's plenty of food, Red-necked Wallabies, which are most active at night, are content to be part of a large mob that feeds on grasses and herbaceous plants. They routinely dine in open areas that are close to forests or woodlands, for these provide a shaded retreat where they can doze during the day and to which they can scurry back and hide if danger creeps too close for comfort while they're out in the open.

In Tasmania, Bennett's Wallabies have found themselves in paradise and have taken advantage of the perfect conditions that have inadvertently been provided for them, for where forests have been destroyed,

grasses have thrived, and with enough trees remaining to keep the wallabies happy, their numbers have increased dramatically in recent decades with an estimated 5 million currently hopping across the state. That's not good news for many farmers however,

Red-necked Wallaby female and joey at Coolah Tops National Park, New South Wales.

and with tens of thousands of Red-necks killed every year by landowners on whose crops they gorge, the news is not too good for the wallabies either.

On the islands of Bass Strait, the wild stretch of ocean between the coast of Victoria and north-western Tasmania, farmers are plagued by immense numbers of wallabies. By conservative estimates, 500,000 call King Island home, and on this speck of land, which is merely 64km long and 26km wide, that equates to around 300 wallabies per square kilometre. Farmers, rather than despairing of the situation, are reaping financial rewards from the growing populations of native animals, with large numbers of wallabies culled every year for their meat.

A similar situation exists on neighbouring Flinders Island, where Bennett's Wallabies have thrived in the absence of any natural predators for more than 20,000 years. Today they graze contentedly on lush pastures that were initially intended for flocks of sheep, and here too their meat provides farmers with a valuable additional source of income.

Death is a sad fact of life, but despite the slaughter, the Bennett's Wallaby remains one of the most commonly seen native animals in Tasmania, and there are plenty of opportunities for human residents of mainland Australia to spot the adorable Red-necked Wallaby too.

# WHIPTAIL WALLABY
*Macropus parryi*

In 1770, when Captain James Cook sailed into the gaping estuary of the Endeavour River in northern Queensland, he spotted a curious animal that, he wrote in his journal, "was of a light mouse colour and the full size of a grey hound, and shaped in every respect like one, with a long tail, which it carried like a grey hound. In short, I should have taken it for a wild dog but for its walking or running, in which it jumped like a hare or deer." "This animal," he added, "is called by the natives, kanguroo."

Joseph Banks, a botanist who accompanied Cook on his voyage of discovery, was equally puzzled by the unfamiliar creature, but he had the opportunity to take a closer look when one of the ship's officers shot the animal that, Banks noted in his journal, "was dressed for our dinners and proved excellent meat." The animal that provided them with valuable sustenance was, in fact, a Whiptail Wallaby.

It's a species that's frequently referred to as a 'pretty-face wallaby,' and there's no question as to the reason behind that colloquial name, for this is a very pretty animal indeed.

It's found only in north-eastern New South Wales and eastern Queensland where, in a range that stretches as far north

Male Whiptail Wallaby near Taroom, Queensland.

as Cooktown, grasslands and woodlands with an understorey of grasses are its favoured habitat.

During the winter months it wears a coat of light grey fur across its back, but in summer it develops a predominantly reddish-brown colouration. It has creamy-white underparts, a prominent similarly coloured hip-stripe and a long slender tail with a thin whip-like end, but it's the Whiptail Wallaby's face that is unquestionably its most attractive feature. Although much of its face is covered with fur of a similar colour to that of its body, it becomes increasingly darker towards the nose, and has wide white cheek-stripes and white fur at the base and near the top of its large ears.

This is the most gregarious of all wallabies and although it's often seen in a small family group, it's frequently part of a large mob. In the heat of the summer they doze among shading vegetation in the middle of the day, but in the cooler months of the year and on overcast summer days they're out and about all day long, feasting on grasses and a wide range of herbaceous plants. They rarely need to drink, except during periods of severe drought, for they obtain all the moisture they require from the vegetation that they eat and from the early morning dew that may be scattered on verdant foliage.

Life is relatively harmonious for Whiptail Wallabies, but during the breeding season there's a hint of aggression instigated by males as they attempt to attract a mate. The mob's dominant male quietly pursues the female that's the focus of his passion, and chases away other males that may have similar intentions to his own. While staring down the opposition, he rips up tufts of grass, presumably in a demonstration of his strength and superiority, and finally wins the day and the right to mate with his chosen partner.

Whip-tail Wallaby at Kroombit Tops National Park, Queensland.

Euro in outback Queensland.

Male Eastern Wallaroo.

# COMMON WALLAROO

*Macropus robustus*

It's easy to be confused about the identification of the wallaroo, for this is an animal that clothes itself in varying attire, with the two major subspecies being dramatically different in their appearance.

The Eastern, Common or Grey Wallaroo rules the slopes of the Great Dividing Range that snakes from north to south down the eastern edge of Australia and divides the moist coastal and hinterland regions from the more arid interior of the continent, while the vast outback regions west of the ranges are the province of another prominent subspecies that's known as the Euro or Red Wallaroo.

The Eastern Wallaroo, which typically has dark grey to black fur, is most at home in cool mountain woodlands and on adjacent steep and rocky hillsides. By contrast, the Euro, which has reddish-brown fur, thrives in arid and semi-arid environments where the stony ridges of ancient and eroded ranges are the predominant feature of the landscape, and where rocky caves and overhangs offer shelter from cold winter nights and from the searing heat of summer. At times they inhabit dense dry scrub and occasionally forage on the plains, but they never stray far from the security of their rugged and stony kingdom.

The Eastern Wallaroo and the Euro have many common physical and behavioural characteristics. Both have thick and shaggy

Eastern Wallaroo at a riverbank camping area north of Bathurst, New South Wales.

Eastern Wallaroo near Scone, New South Wales.

fur, with the colour, which is always lighter on females, varying considerably and, particularly in the case of the Euro, often being similar to that of the primary colour of the landscape. Adult males are exceptionally stocky with their strong and muscular forearms giving them the appearance of the tough guys of the neighbourhood, and all animals of both subspecies have underparts that are lighter than the colour of the fur on their back, a hairless black nose, large pale-coloured ears and a very thick tail.

They're generally solitary creatures, but when there's an abundance of food they congregate in groups, and during the coolest parts of the day and throughout the night they browse on grasses and the foliage of a wide range of shrubs.

Euros require less water than the kangaroos of the outback plains and they know all the tricks of survival that are demanded by their often harsh environment. They seek out vegetation that has a high moisture content, and they select the coolest and most humid areas in which to wile away the hottest hours of the day. With the ability to locate underground water in seemingly dry creek beds, they scratch at the surface to reach the life-giving fluid and are thus less dependant than other species of macropods on surface water that rapidly evaporates under summer's searing gaze. They have one other unique ploy to ensure their survival. They recycle urea through their saliva, rather than excrete it in their urine, and thus have a reduced demand for nitrogen, and with less of their body's water lost through urination, they're able to retain water to assist in keeping cool and can thrive in the most hostile environments where only mad dogs and Englishmen venture out in the midday sun.

Euro in outback South Australia.

Above and opposite: Grey-headed Flying-foxes at Hervey Bay, Queensland.

# OTHER MAMMALS

Australia is home to more than 380 species of mammals, many of which are marsupials that give birth to relatively undeveloped young that the mother carries in a pouch as they grow. With approximately 70 per cent of the world's marsupial species found in Australia, this is unquestionably the lucky country.

## GREY-HEADED FLYING-FOX
*Pteropus poliocephalus*

In recent years an aura of fear has surrounded the Grey-headed Flying-fox, for flying-foxes are carriers of the Hendra virus that made its first appearance in 1994. It's horses that are primarily at risk from this usually fatal disease, and although some 70 horses and four people have died after contracting the disease, there's no evidence of humans having been directly infected by contact with flying-foxes, and there's no genuine reason to fear these creatures of the night.

Grey-headed Flying-foxes inhabit eastern Australia, from Rockhampton in central Queensland to western Victoria, and in recent years they've ventured further west towards Adelaide in South Australia. They make themselves at home wherever there's a supply of their favoured foods, which include the nectar and pollen of flowering trees, in addition to fruit, and they hang around in forests, woodlands, orchards and urban parks and gardens.

The Grey-headed Flying-fox's name refers to its facial resemblance to a Red Fox, and although its head is covered with grey fur, the fur that coats its chest and its back is of the same chestnut-brown colouration as its terrestrial namesake. With a wingspan of up to a metre, these are the largest bats in Australia and among the largest in the world. They are highly social nocturnal animals that, during the day, hang out together, suspended among the branches of trees, in flocks that can contain several thousand individuals. With their dark grey

Grey-headed Flying-foxes at Hervey Bay, Queensland.

they visit, but when natural foods are scarce, they have no qualms about feeding on the sweet and succulent fruits of orchards, and consequently make themselves very unpopular.

As the warmth of summer approaches, females give birth to a single young that, for the first few weeks of its life, clings tenaciously to its mother's body, but when it's time for the tiny bat to taste independence, it's left to hang out for the night in a creche with other juveniles while their parents head off to feed.

The population of Grey-headed Flying-foxes has declined dramatically in recent decades, and they're currently listed as a vulnerable species. They once numbered in their millions, but there are now around 600,000, and while that figure may not give everyone cause for concern, the future of these great bats could be grim if the rate of decline that has been seen in recent years continues unabated.

There's no doubt that many people would welcome a reduction in their population, for when they congregate in immense numbers, fouling the ground beneath their roosting sites, creating an overpowering stench, and shattering any hint of tranquillity with their incessant screeching, they make themselves far from welcome, and despite the fact that they play an invaluable role in the environment, no one wants flying-foxes hanging around on their doorstep.

wings wrapped tightly around their bodies, it's a time when workers on the night shift should be sleeping, but there's always plenty of argy-bargy going on in a colony of flying-foxes, and peace and quiet is rarely the order of the day as they flutter and squawk in their arboreal roosts.

At dusk, there's an even greater crescendo of noise as they head off to their favoured feeding grounds. They'll travel up to 50km in search of the best place to dine, and will enthusiastically feast on the flowers of native trees, including eucalypts, banksias and melaleucas. They play an important role by pollinating the flowers of each tree that

This Greater Glider was discovered in the author's garden after the tree that had been its home crashed to the ground during a storm.

# GREATER GLIDER
*Petauroides volans*

This stunningly beautiful nocturnal animal is rarely seen by human eyes. It glides silently through the darkness from one tree to another and, if the need arises, it can change direction abruptly while in flight, and it does so with the greatest of ease, thanks to the strong flaps of skin that connect its front and hind legs, and that act like wings to allow this agile aviator to move secretively through its lofty realm.

The woodlands and eucalypt forests of eastern Australia, from northern Queensland to central Victoria, are the

Greater Gliders' domain, and what they require for their survival are large trees with hollows in which they can spend each day in the land of nod.

They are the largest of Australia's arboreal gliders and have thick dark grey or brown fur covering much of the body, a light brown face, creamy-white throat and chest, long furry tail and large furry ears.

Populations vary considerably across their range with conspicuous variations in colour and size. In 2020 researchers analysed the DNA of several animals and discovered that the Greater Glider was, in fact, not one species but three. The newly named Petauroides minor, the species that inhabits the forests of northern Queensland, is the size of a small Ringtail Possum, while Petauroides volans, the cat-sized species that's illustrated here, is found south of the Tropic of Capricorn. The third species, Petauroides armillatus, inhabits the forests of the Great Dividing Range to the west of the Queensland city of Mackay and north to Townsville.

Greater Gliders feed almost exclusively on the leaves of a few species of eucalyptus trees, but will also eat the trees' flowers and buds, and when they opt for a change of taste they'll nibble on the leaves of acacias and on the parasitic mistletoe that often drapes itself across the limbs of eucalyptus trees.

For much of the year they live a solitary existence, but each is content to share its treetop accommodation with a mate when the breeding season arrives. Females give birth to a single young that travels with its mother, in the comfort and security of her pouch, for the first 3–4 months of its life. As it savours independence, it waits in a treetop hollow or clings to its mother's back while she forages for food, but the youngster draws the line at hanging on tight while its mother flies through the air. At about 10 months of age it takes a great leap of confidence and soars through the forest on its first courageous flight.

In the Greater Gliders' habitat there's keen competition for tree hollows, with other gliders, possums and many species of birds all requiring similar accommodation. They'll fiercely defend their home range and any hollows to which they claim ownership, but there's little they can do other than flee for their lives when a large owl, goanna, snake or other hungry predator arrives on the scene.

Populations of Greater Gliders have been in decline for many years with habitat loss from bushfires, land clearing and the logging of old-growth forests creating a very real threat to their long-term survival. Since the beginning of the 21st century their numbers have declined by 80 per cent, Despite being listed as 'vulnerable' in 2016, habitat destruction continued unabated, and in 2022 the Greater Glider's classification was changed to 'endangered'.

Brushtail possum at a camping area in Bournda National Park, New South Wales.

Brushtail possums are perfectly adapted to an arboreal life.

# COMMON BRUSHTAIL POSSUM

*Trichosurus vulpecula*

Common Brushtail Possums, which are found in all states of Australia, are nocturnal marsupials that live in woodlands and forests where they spend their days sleeping on shaded branches or in hollows in old trees, but they've found a new world to inhabit and have enthusiastically moved into urban environments where humans generously, although often unwittingly, provide everything that possums require for their survival. When they seek more upmarket accommodation, they'll take up residence in a dark corner of a garden shed or garage, or become squatters in the roof cavity of a house.

In the wild, they supplement their diet of fruit with snacks of leaves and flowers, but in suburbia there's a far wider range of goodies on offer than at Mother Nature's table. Fruit is still at the top of the possums' menu, and they'll happily gorge themselves on any that they find in backyards and commercial orchards. They'll feast on a range of other tasty treats too, including garden vegetables,

These young twin brushtail possums were born and raised in the author's garden shed.

Brushtail possum feeding.

pink nose and pink toes with large claws, the brushtail possum is a beautiful animal. It spends much of its life alone, but when an individual discovers a convenient urban habitat, others often move in to share the accommodation. After a night of carousing and feeding they return, just before dawn, to settle down to sleep, and those that have found shelter in the roof of a house make their presence known to the building's human inhabitants with angry growling as disputes erupt over the sleeping arrangements.

There's plenty of argy-bargy too when the breeding season arrives, and they hiss and growl as males fight for the right to mate with the female of their choice. Females usually give birth to a single young, although occasionally twins are born, and the tiny baby, with legs no thicker than a blade of straw, struggles through its mother's dense fur to reach her pouch where it remains safe and warm for several months. Later, it rides on her back, gradually acquiring all the skills it will require to survive in an urban jungle or a native forest.

Possums were once hunted for their soft fur and were in demand by early settlers as bush tucker to add to a steaming stew, but in the modern era, with Lady Luck as their companion, a comfortable life is guaranteed if they can evade the gaping jaws of dingoes, cats, foxes and pythons that are always on the lookout for a meal.

flowers and foliage, and are particularly partial to roses, and will devour the entire plant, including its flowers, leaves, stems and thorns.

With its body covered in grey to brown fur, and with large ears, a long furry tail,

# KOALA
*Phascolarctos cinereus*

Koala in the woodlands of Raymond Island, Victoria.

The Koala's earliest ancestors are believed to have existed more than 25 million years ago, but they were twice the size of the cuddly character that, in 1798, left John Price wide-eyed with amazement. He was a member of a group that was exploring the land beyond Sydney, and claimed his moment of fame as the first European to record a sighting of a Koala.

In that distant era, huge numbers of Koalas thrived in the continent's extensive eucalypt woodlands, but their luxurious fur made them a prime target for hunters. By the early years of the 20th century, their populations had been decimated in South Australia, New South Wales and Victoria, and Queensland became the new hunting ground for those who supplied the fur trade. In 1919, when the state government announced a six-month open season on the animals, an estimated 1 million were slaughtered, and in 1927, during another hunting season, 800,000 were massacred in a single month. An outcry of public indignation finally led to the Koala being listed as a protected species in 1937.

An estimated 80,000 Koalas live in eastern Australia, with their range extending from northern Queensland to central and western areas of the state, and into New South

Wales, Victoria and South Australia, but with the continual destruction of their habitat, and with disease and predators putting additional pressure on their populations, there are grave concerns for the remaining communities of these iconic animals.

Koalas, which are primarily nocturnal, survive on a diet of nothing more than eucalyptus leaves, and although these are extremely fibrous and have low levels of nutrients, Koalas are perfectly adapted to such a monotonous and low quality diet. The half a kilo or more of leaves that an adult Koala eats every night provides only a minimal amount of energy, so rather than go gallivanting around, they sleep for around 18 hours a day to conserve their energy.

A mature male is readily distinguished by the prominent brown patch on the white fur of his chest. It's a sticky substance that's exuded from his scent gland, and it's this that he rubs onto trees to ensure that other Koalas are well aware that they're within his territory. A female with which he's mated gives birth to a tiny naked joey that, despite being blind and merely 20mm long, makes a miraculous journey through its mother's dense fur to her pouch where it remains for approximately 6 months until it's confident enough to clamber outside and ride on its mother's back or cling to her abdomen.

Koalas rarely need to drink for they obtain sufficient moisture from their food, and usually clamber down to the ground only when they want to move from one tree to another. It's then that they're most vulnerable to predators, and are also at risk of being injured or killed as they venture, with their curious waddling gait, across roads. Their natural predators include large reptiles, dingoes and birds of prey, but Koalas are most at risk from dogs, and also from vehicles that are responsible for the deaths of around 4,000 of these animals every year.

Some 80 per cent of Australia's eucalypt forests have been destroyed or have become severely fragmented since the first days of European settlement, and as areas of prime habitat continue to fall victim to human progress, the Koala, which is listed as an endangered species, continues its dawdling journey along the road that leads towards extinction.

Since 2001, Queensland's Koala population has declined by 50 per cent and in New South Wales the situation is even more disastrous with numbers having declined by a staggering 65 per cent. A recent New South Wales parliamentary committee report relating to the state of Koala populations and habitats found that, without significant government intervention, these iconic animals will become extinct in New South Wales by 2050, and with every tree that is destroyed that grim prophecy is nudged closer to reality.

Echidna on outback plains near Cunnamulla, Queensland.

## SHORT-BEAKED ECHIDNA
*Tachyglossus aculeatus*

The Short-beaked Echidna is unques-tionably a most peculiar animal, for it's one of only two types of monotremes, egg-laying mammals, which exist anywhere on Earth, and it's a claim to fame that it shares only with the Platypus.

It's one of Australia's most widespread native mammals and can be found through-out the continent. Echidnas make themselves at home in a diverse range of environments, from snow-covered mountains to semi-arid outback regions, providing there are hollow logs or rocky crevices in which they can shelter during the sizzling summer heat and on icy winter days.

Echidnas have long, sharp spines cover-ing the back of their short and stocky bodies, and almost inconspicuous tails. Their short legs are perfectly designed for digging, with their front feet having claws that enable them to dig into decaying logs and termite mounds in search of food, while their hind feet point backwards and allow them to push soil away when they're burrowing.

This amazing animal, which is commonly

Echidna in bushland north of Sydney, New South Wales.

referred to as a 'spiny anteater' utilises elec-troreceptors on its long, tubular snout to detect danger, find a mate, and search for food as it rummages through debris on the forest floor or shuffles through the grasses of the open plains that it also inhabits. It excavates termite mounds with its strong claws, and probes every crevice with its long tongue. At times it takes the lazy option, and after scraping away the crust of a termite mound to send its inhabitants into a frenzy, the echidna simply lies on the mound and waits for the termites to walk onto its extended tongue. It takes more than a few to satisfy its appetite, but an echidna can devour 200 grams of its favoured insects in merely 10 minutes.

It's a timid creature that's out and about both day and night and that, when startled by the approach of a human or in an attempt to evade a predator, will tuck its snout and legs beneath its body to create a spiny ball, dig itself into soft soil, squeeze into a crevice among rocks, or simply waddle away in an ungainly hurry.

Echidnas, which are generally solitary

animals, come together only to mate. During the breeding season, the female develops a pouch into which she lays a single egg that eventually cracks open to reveal a tiny animal that's about 15mm long. The young echidna, known as a puggle, remains in its mother's pouch for about three months, sucking milk from mammary hairs, but as its spines begin to develop, it's evicted from the pouch and raised in a shallow burrow until, at about six months of age, it sets out alone to face the world.

Despite their formidable armour, echidnas are frequently stalked by hungry dingoes and foxes that have developed ways of coping with even the most prickly of prey. Many fall victim to the appetites of these ravenous carnivores, but with luck on their side echidnas can live to the grand old age of 45.

An orphaned echidna puggle in the hands of a wildlife carer.

Dainty Green Tree Frog in the author's garden.

# FROGS

While some of the approximately 200 species of frogs that are endemic to Australia have enthusiastically adapted to an urban environment, others face the threat of extinction due primarily to the impact of diseases and the destruction of their natural habitat.

The loss of a single species may be considered as another small hop in the decline of the biodiversity of the region and elicit sadness at the thought that future generations will never have the opportunity to see one of Mother Nature's unique creations, but the extinction of even a single species may prove to be a loss not only for Australians, but for all of humanity.

The secretions that are exuded from the skins of all frogs have been found to have antifungal and antibacterial properties that provide protection from the fungal, viral and bacterial diseases that exist in the specific environment that each species inhabits. That's a genuinely good news story, for researchers are confident that some of these secretions may aid in the creation of new drugs that will combat human diseases, including cancer, diabetes and cardiovascular disease, and with the secretions from Australian Green Tree Frogs having already been shown to inhibit HIV infection, there's every reason to be confident that medical miracles may not be far away.

Green Tree Frogs make themselves at home in the patio of the author's house.

Above and opposite: Green Tree Frog in the author's garden.

## GREEN TREE FROG
*Litoria caerulea*

The Green Tree Frog was the first Australian frog to be scientifically described, and the honour of bringing this colourful amphibian to the attention of the world was claimed by British naval surgeon John White who arrived in Australia with the first fleet in 1788 and established the country's first hospital in the fledgling colony.

Today, it's still occasionally referred to as 'White's Tree Frog,' and although his experiences brought John White a touch of fame, he couldn't wait to hightail it out of Australia, which he referred to in his journal as "a country and place so forbidding and so hateful as only to merit execration and curses."

He returned to England in 1794 and his original amphibian specimen found its way into the vast collection of the illustrious botanist Joseph Banks and, when it finally arrived in London, it was given the species name *caerulea*, a derivation of a Latin word meaning 'blue.' Why, you might ask, would anyone with even a touch more sanity than a demented bed bug christen a green frog with such a name? The simple answer is that the creature had been preserved in alcohol that had altered the colour of its skin. Strange as it might seem, living Green Tree Frogs are occasionally blue too, due to a lack of yellow pigmentation, while others that, with no blue pigmentation, have yellow colouration, are also occasionally discovered.

The Green Tree Frog is one of the most common of all Australian frogs and is found in most eastern regions of the mainland, with the exception of Victoria. It lives in damp forests, woodlands and wetlands, and has enthusiastically adapted to life in many urban environments. When it opts to call a human's residence its home, it makes itself

comfortable in gutters and downpipes, in cool and damp areas around water tanks, and under the eaves of houses where it hides during the day in dark and shaded corners.

With adults growing up to 11cm in length, it's one of Australia's largest frogs, and with its distinctively rounded head, a prominent fold of skin above each 'ear,' golden-yellow eyes, typically bright green colouration, a cream belly, and thighs that, on the underside, are yellow, pink or red, it's one of the most recognisable of all amphibians. It has the ability to change the colour of its skin from vibrant green to more drab olive hues or even brown to match its surroundings and thus adopt a hint of camouflage that allows it to remain concealed from predators. When, in its urban home, it settles down to spend the day behind outdoor furniture, behind a hanging picture on a patio wall, among flowerpots or behind the curtains of an open window, the Green Tree Frog is the most invisible of visitors.

On spring and summer nights males give their presence away with their loud and repetitive voices as they summon a mate, and *croak, croak, croak* echoes from drains and downpipes, from ornamental pools and from clumps of damp vegetation.

When it's food rather than sex that's on the Green Tree Frog's mind, it will spend the night catching insects that are drawn to lights, and hunting its prey on illuminated windows. When a more substantial meal comes within reach, it will enthusiastically feed on mice and small reptiles, such as geckos, that also share the homes of many Australians.

Green Tree Frogs are routinely in danger of becoming the main course for snakes and other reptiles, but they don't succumb to such threats quietly. When danger rears its head they let out a shrill, blood-curdling scream that does little to deter an attacker, yet brings startled humans rushing to see what all the commotion is about.

In the first months of summer they lay their eggs, which are encased in a mass of transparent jelly, in calm water, and a swarm of wriggling tadpoles eventually hatches, with development from an egg to a tiny froglet taking around six weeks.

These frogs are relatively long-lived, with the oldest recorded captive specimen surviving to the wrinkled old age of 23. Those in the wild have shorter lives however, and their population, like that of many other species, has declined in recent years. Frogs play a vital role in the health and maintenance of many ecosystems, for they assist in controlling populations of insects and provide food for other species of wildlife. With a small and inexpensive garden water feature it's easy to create the perfect environment to give these appealing little creatures a helping hand in their ongoing battle for survival.

A Peron's Tree Frog regularly makes itself at home on the patio of the author's house.

## PERON'S TREE FROG
*Litoria peronii*

This tiny frog bears the name of Francois Peron, a zoologist who accompanied Frenchman Nicolas Baudin on his expedition to map the western and southern coasts of Australia in 1800–1804.

It's found in northern Victoria, New South Wales and southern Queensland, with its favoured habitats being within forests where it lives, often well away from any major source of water, in hollows in trees and under flaking bark, but like many other frogs it has adopted urban areas as part of its habitat.

It grows to a length of merely 5cm, but this diminutive amphibian packs some big surprises, for like a chameleon it can rapidly change the colour of its distinctively warty skin. During daylight hours the majority of its body is light grey, brown or drab olive-green, with the only highlight being the black and yellow markings on its thighs and armpits, but at night it puts on more ornate garb of reddish brown that's enhanced with specks of emerald green, and it's this touch of bling that has earned Peron's Tree Frog the alternative common name of 'Emerald-spotted Tree Frog.'

It reveals its presence, particularly when it's searching for a mate, with a curious, high-pitched cackling sound. When females are ready to breed, they seek out water in which to lay their eggs. The still waters of wetlands, farm dams, waterholes and garden fishponds are exactly what they're looking for, and in no time at all, hordes of yellowish-green tadpoles are wriggling around in their aquatic home and, as each moment passes, the day that they will evolve into tiny froglets comes a little closer.

Above and opposite: Dainty Green Tree Frog in the author's garden.

## DAINTY GREEN TREE FROG

*Litoria gracilenta*

The Dainty Green Tree Frog is a resident of eastern Australia where it's found in wetlands and in moist woodland and forest environments in an area that stretches from northern Queensland to central New South Wales. Like many other frogs, it's more than happy to settle into an urban environment if there are cool and damp areas, and sources of water where it can deposit its eggs.

This tiny frog, which is merely 4–5cm in length, is one of Australia's great travellers, and it's often discovered in fruit shops and supermarkets after hitching a ride among a bunch of bananas transported from northern growing areas. It's the little stowaway's regular jaunts that have earned it the colloquial name of 'banana frog.'

Although the Dainty Green Tree Frog, which has rough textured skin, is often bright green, many individuals have an absence of blue pigmentation and thus have golden-yellow skin, which provides this diminutive creature with the perfect camouflage it requires to hide among ripening fruit. Its most distinguishing feature, one that sets it apart from other similarly coloured small frogs, is the pale yellow stripe that stretches from each nostril to each ear, and this, together with its golden-yellow eyes, ensures that the Dainty Green Tree Frog is among the most attractive of amphibians.

Beneath the protective cloak of night, it hunts for the insects that are its primary source of food, but during the day, this colourful little frog sits silently on a leaf or on other vegetation, and with its legs and partially webbed feet tucked neatly into the sides of its body, it becomes almost invisible.

During the coolest months of the year it's happy to live well away from water, but it's a different story when the mercury rises, for it's then that the urge to breed dominates the lives of these appealing little frogs. It's not vast lakes and sprawling rivers that they require however, for all each needs is a mate and a small pool of water. Females lay their eggs in puddles of water in grasslands, shallow waterholes, and garden ponds, and attach their valuable deposits to the submerged stems of grasses or other vegetation. The dark brown tadpoles that eventually hatch  take around 14 weeks to develop into the small frogs that are the wildlife emblem of the Queensland city of Brisbane. Being so small though, the Dainty Green Tree Frog is a creature that many of the city's human inhabitants have never seen, although it's often right on their doorstep.

## STRIPED MARSH FROG
*Limnodynastes peronii*

The highly distinctive Striped Marsh Frog can be found from northern Queensland to northern Tasmania, although it's relatively rare in the most southerly parts of its range.

*Limnodynastes*, the name of the genus to which it belongs, gives a clue as to where this tiny creature resides, for it's a word that owes

Striped Marsh Frogs thrive in the ponds in the author's garden.

its origins to the Greek *limno*, meaning a marsh, and the Latin *dynastes*, which means a ruler. The Striped Marsh Frog is true to its name, for although it thrives in forests and woodlands that are close to a permanent source of water, it's marshes and wetlands that are at the heart of its kingdom.

Almost any source of calm water, from a wetland lagoon to a farm dam, and even the stagnant water in a roadside ditch, is prime real estate as far as the ruler of the marshes is concerned, and this highly adaptable little frog is also more than happy to take up residence in an urban environment, providing there's a pond that it can claim as its personal domain.

The Striped Marsh Frog, which measures 6–7cm in length when fully grown, has alternating dark and light brown stripes along the length of its body, and a narrower pale brown stripe running from its pointed head along the centre of its back. Its light brown head is adorned with a wide dark brown strip that runs from the nostril, beyond the eye, and to the top of the foreleg, with a parallel pale stripe below it. The sides of its body are light brown with irregularly shaped chocolate brown spots and patches, and its belly is creamy-brown to white. It has feet that have no webbing but that have exceptionally long toes, particularly on the hind-feet.

During the day, particularly in the winter months, they're about as lively as the participants at an annual gathering of tortoises, for they spend their time taking it easy under logs and rocks, or dozing among dense vegetation at the water's edge, but as the sun slithers towards the horizon, the urge to hunt for food prompts them into action. Although insects routinely satisfy their appetites, Striped Marsh Frogs are skilful and efficient hunters and will eat almost anything smaller than themselves, and that includes other species of frogs.

Males have stocky muscular forearms, and in late winter and spring, when they have more than food on their minds, they get down to some serious arm-to-arm combat, with the strongest males defeating their rivals and winning the right to mate with the most desirable females. Each female lays several hundred eggs in a mass of jelly that she creates on the surface of the water. Almost any water will do, and the Striped Marsh Frog's less-than-fussy attitude sees her occasionally lay her eggs in a dog's water bowl or in a garden bird bath where the chances of survival for her young are about as slim as the possibility of seeing a fish knitting a pair of socks.

The male, after doing his bit to ensure the survival of his species, has plenty to shout about, and his distinctive nocturnal call, a loud and slowly repeated *tok*, is a clear indication that the Striped Marsh Frog remains the ruler of his little corner of the world.

# CANE TOAD

*Rhinella marina* syn. *Bufo marinus*

In 1935, Cane Toads, a species that originated in southern areas of the USA and tropical parts of Latin America, were introduced into Australia with the promise that they would assist in the battle to control beetles that, with their larvae feeding on the roots of sugar cane, were the scourge of the sugar cane industry. Little attention was given to the concerns of scientists who protested against the introduction of these alien creatures, but they would be turning in their graves if they could see that their worst nightmares have become reality.

The toads had no significant impact on populations of the destructive beetles, and it soon became evident that the amphibian which had arrived with the promise of a miracle had become a curse of monumental intensity.

Today, Cane Toads thrive in a wide range of habitats, including rainforests, freshwater and coastal swamps, grasslands and woodlands, and will set up home in any urban area that's within their ever-expanding range. This invasive pest, having spread throughout eastern Queensland, has made its way south into New South Wales, hopped into the Northern Territory, and recently arrived in the north of Western Australia. As Cane Toads colonise the river systems of western Queensland, the fear is that they may eventually make their way south, via inland waterways, to South Australia.

The Cane Toad, which only another member of its own species could see as an attractive creature, has brown mottled and warty skin on its upper body, creamy-brown underparts, a prominent bony ridge between its nostrils and its eyes, and webbed feet.

While most native frogs are primarily creatures of the night, Cane Toads are relatively active during daylight hours, particularly on warm and rainy days when they emerge from their hiding places under rocks and logs and among dense vegetation, and sit patiently, in a typically upright pose, beside tiny holes in the ground. With a rapid flick of the tongue, they gorge themselves on hordes of flying ants that emerge from their subterranean world. Cane Toads devour a wide range of other insects too, in addition to mice, small reptiles, frogs and carrion, and will even supplement their diet with dog food if Fido's left his meal unattended for more than a moment or two.

In common with other amphibians, the Cane Toad is both a hunter and the prey of other hungry creatures, but the secret to its survival is the toxin that it secretes from its skin and that, when threatened, is also released from glands at the back of its head. It's poisonous at every stage of its life, with fish that eat the toad's tadpoles enjoying the last meal of their lives, and animals that consume adult toads almost inevitably condemned to death.

The toads head for a source of water when they're ready to breed, and they're very easy to please, for any still water, whether fresh, stagnant or slightly saline, in anything from a shallow and murky pool to a lake or a garden pond, will suit them to perfection. A female can lay more than 33,000 eggs in a season, and unlike the eggs of native frogs, her brood are laid in long thin strands of transparent jelly that are tangled around aquatic plants.

The introduction of the Cane Toad was unquestionably one of the worst disasters that Australians have inflicted on the environment. Its impact on many species of wildlife, particularly those whose existence is already under threat, has been considerable, but some wild creatures are adapting to cope with the danger that the Cane Toad has brought to their world. Some birds have learnt to feed on toads without suffering any ill effects, for they flip their prey onto its back and rip at the soft skin of its underbelly to expose and eat its innards, thus avoiding contact with the toad's deadly poison. And Keelback Snakes can scoff Cane Toads with what appears to be immunity.

With scientists unable to discover any safe and effective method to control the spread of this unwelcome invader, it will be left to Mother Nature to prove her resilience and ingenuity and, with her offsider Evolution, she may ultimately win the war and lead Australia's wild creatures to victory over this silent and stealthy enemy.

Cane Toad in the author's garden.

Above and opposite: Water Dragon at Bundaberg Botanic Gardens, Queensland.

# REPTILES

Australia is home to more than 860 species of reptiles and can boast of being the only continent where venomous snakes outnumber non-venomous ones, and of having more species of lizards than any other country. It's also home to the world's largest reptile, the Saltwater Crocodile, which being more than 6m in length and weighing a tonne is a fearsome beast that no one would like to encounter on their doorstep.

## WATER DRAGON
*Intellagama lesueurii*

Water Dragons are found in eastern Australia in an extensive area that stretches from northern Queensland to south-eastern New South Wales and eastern Victoria. As the name suggests, water is central to their lifestyle, and they're content to spend their lives in habitats as diverse as tropical rainforests, alpine bushland and urban parklands, providing there's a river, a gentle stream or a lake on the doorstep.

Fossils have revealed that close relatives of the Water Dragon thrived in what is now the state of Queensland more than 20 million years ago, and it's easy to accept that link to the past, for this largest of Australia's dragon lizards, which can reach a length of 90cm, has a distinctive resemblance to the

Juvenile Water Dragon in the author's garden.

dinosaurs that once ruled the Earth.

Its head, legs and body are brown to grey with dark brown to black flecks, spots and stripes, and it has a long tail with similar colouration that will regrow if severed. With spiny scales on its head and neck, a prominent jagged ridge along its back, and large claws on its toes, the Water Dragon, particularly an adult male with its vivid orange chest, may appear to be a rather intimidating creature, but that's an illusion, for this relatively timid reptile poses no threat to humans.

Juveniles feed entirely on insects, but their tastes change as they mature, and although adults will happily eat small fish and crustaceans such as yabbies, and insects that they catch while foraging among the foliage of trees, they also like their fruit and veggies, with leaves, fruit and flowers making up more than 50 per cent of their diet.

During the coldest months of the year Water Dragons retreat to burrows abandoned by rabbits or other animals, or excavate a shelter among boulders or logs that are close to a watercourse. After sealing themselves in with a barricade of dirt, they slow down their metabolism and doze in a state of brumation, the reptilian equivalent of seasonal hibernation that's practiced by some mammal species, until spring arrives.

When the weather warms up, they bask on sunlit logs and rocks, and on branches overhanging rivers and streams, and if a predator or a curious human wanders too close for comfort, they simply run at great speed into dense vegetation or, as efficient swimmers and with an ability to remain submerged for almost an hour, they may leap into the water and vanish from sight in less time that it takes for a flea to jump from one scratching mongrel to another. It's often only a splash and a ripple on the surface as they dive into the water that gives their presence away.

Warm weather triggers the urge to breed, and each female, after mating, eventually excavates a hole in sandy soil and lays her clutch of 6–18 eggs. The hatchlings are at the mercy of numerous predators, including snakes, and with adults occasionally harbouring cannibalistic tendencies, the life of a young Water Dragon was never meant to be easy.

Water Dragon at Bundaberg Botanic Gardens, Queensland.

Feasting on a stick insect.

Water Dragon with fish prey.

With body inflated in threat posture.

# EASTERN BEARDED DRAGON

*Pogona barbata*

To many people the Eastern Bearded Dragon is an ugly and terrifying creature, but to others, particularly those whose gardens are regularly visited by this spiny lizard, it's a reptile that's always welcome.

It owes its name to the spiny flap of skin under its chin that it extends, when threatened, to make it appear larger and more ferocious than it really is. If that isn't enough to deter any threat, it inflates its body, and displays a gaping yellow mouth in a demonstration of silent aggression that generally convinces both predators and humans that this is a wild beastie that's best left alone. If its aggressive pose doesn't

Bearded dragon in the author's garden.

have the desired effect, the Eastern Bearded Dragon has speed and agility as its ultimate survival options, and it runs at astonishing speed into dense vegetation or up the trunk of the nearest tree to escape from danger.

These lizards, which grow to a length of around 60cm, are relatively common in eastern Australia, from northern Queensland to New South Wales, northern Victoria and south-eastern South Australia. With their mottled grey to brown colouration, they're perfectly camouflaged in the eucalypt forests and woodlands of their natural habitat where they spend much of their time sitting motionlessly on logs or rocks, warming themselves in the sunlight, or waiting for a takeaway meal to wander past.

Young Eastern Bearded Dragons feast almost entirely on insects, but with age comes a new diet that's based primarily on fruit and vegetation, although adults add insects, small reptiles, mice and frogs to the menu if fruit is in short supply. They quench their thirst not by drinking from pools of water but by lapping up the morning dew or raindrops from leaves.

These spiny creatures pose no threat to humans, but males can be highly aggressive, particularly towards other males that may intrude into their territory. Females are welcome however, and after mating each digs a shallow hole in the soil and lays a clutch of 10–30 eggs. When the eggs eventually hatch, the tiny reptiles are on their own, and if food and appropriate habitat are available, there's a good chance that some of these curious reptiles will make themselves at home in an urban environment.

Feeding on fallen fruit.

Bearded dragon in the author's garden.

Above and opposite: Shingleback in a threat pose, outback South Australia.

# SHINGLEBACK
*Tiliqua rugosa*

It's hard to image that any animal could have a wider range of common names than this large and distinctive skink, for in addition to being known as a Shingleback, it's also frequently referred to as a 'bobtail', 'blue-tongue', 'stumpy-tail', 'sleepy lizard' and 'two-headed skink'.

It's a lizard that inhabits the arid and semi-arid regions of the continent, with its range including inland areas of southern Queensland and New South Wales, Victoria, eastern South Australia and southern Western Australia, where its favoured haunts are in deserts and sand dunes daubed with drought-tolerant grasses.

The thick scales of its armour can be in varying shades of brown, with its underparts usually of a lighter hue. It has a triangular pointed head, a body that's around 30cm in length, and a short rounded tail that's of similar shape to its head – a feature that sometimes confuses predators that fail to recognise which end of this curious creature is which.

With its short legs it's a reptile that usually travels at a speed rivalling that of a snake in Antarctica, and that means that it has to take the easy option when searching for food, and feasts on snails, carrion, flowers and leaves that also are going nowhere in a hurry.

Dingoes, cats, foxes and some species of snakes are not intimidated by the sight of the Shingleback's armour, but when a prospective meal presents them with a gaping red mouth and a large blue tongue, most predators think again and may consider that retreat from what appears to be a terrifying beast is the best option.

When warm weather triggers an interest in the opposite sex, Shinglebacks seek out a familiar companion, for these are monogamous reptiles that mate with the same partner every year. Each female gives birth to live young, with each litter comprising 5–24 babies that remain with their parents for several months.

When winter inevitably approaches once again, the slow pace of life of a Shingleback comes almost to a standstill as each settles into a sheltered burrow and slows down its metabolism as it enters a state of brumation, which is similar to hibernation in mammals. Thanks to the reserves of fat that are retained in their stumpy tails, they survive, concealed from the world and its countless dangers, until spring makes its welcome return.

## MORITZ'S LEAF-TAILED GECKO

*Saltuarius moritzi*

The Moritz's Leaf-tailed Gecko is a secretive creature that lives in the humid forests of north-eastern New South Wales, with its limited range, which lies to the south of the Clarence River, stretching west from the forests of the coastal zone to those of the Great Dividing Range and the New England tablelands.

This curious reptile is the most widespread of the 16 species of leaf-tailed geckos that are found only in eastern Australia, but it's not easy to see in its natural habitat where it's as perfectly camouflaged as a rusting nail in the rotting timbers of a derelict outback dunny.

Its highly variable grey to brown colouration, which is enhanced with decorative patterns in varying shades of brown, and its large and distinctive leaf-shaped tail ensure that only those who enter its dark and forested world with patience, keen eyesight

Moritz's Leaf-tailed Gecko on the wall of a toilet block at a camping area near Dorrigo, New South Wales.

and luck as their companions will be treated to a glimpse of this elusive creature that grows to a length of around 10cm.

This highly ornate gecko, with its common name honouring Professor Craig Moritz for his contribution to knowledge regarding rainforest reptiles, is a nocturnal lizard that feasts on a range of smaller creatures, including insects and spiders. In common with other geckos, its tail regenerates if damaged, it uses its tongue to clean the clear coverings over its lidless eyes, and it emits a squeaking sound when threatened or when cavorting with a mate.

After mating, each female lays two tiny eggs that, if the hatchlings evade predators, will give this unique species another opportunity to enthral all who see it.

## BURTON'S SNAKE-LIZARD

*Lialis burtonis*

Hopefully Edward Burton was never legless at work, for he was a 19th-century British army surgeon who saw some dreadful sights that would, no doubt, have triggered the urge for a stiff drink. The lizard that was named in Doctor Burton's honour is permanently legless as a result of evolution's handiwork, for over aeons its legs have become barely visible features of its anatomy and are now nothing more than scaly flaps. It's these that have earned Burton's Snake-lizard its alternative common name of 'flap-footed lizard.'

As Australia's most widespread reptile

Burton's Snake-lizard in the author's garden.

it thrives in most regions of the mainland, with the exception of the south-western coast, south-eastern Victoria and southern New South Wales. It makes itself at home among the sandy ridges of arid and semi-arid inland regions, on stony desert plains, and in woodlands and dry forests, and it lives on the doorstep of cities where pockets of urban bushland provide it with suitable habitat. However rainforests, the highest and coolest sectors of the Great Dividing Range, and urban areas that have been stripped clear of all native vegetation are definitely not within its comfort zone.

Growing to a length of more than 60cm, it's one of the largest of Australia's 42 species of legless lizards. With a long slender body and a long and pointed head, it's a most distinctive creature, with individuals, even those living within the same area, often having dramatically different colours and patterns to those displayed by their neigh-bours. They can have cream to grey or even reddish-brown bodies and tails with stripes, spots or no pattern at all, other than the dark brown to black stripes that many have on their face and on the first part of their body.

Like the geckos to which they are closely related, legless lizards use their tongues to clean the clear coverings of their lidless eyes. They make distinctive squeaking sounds when threatened and during social encounters, and their tails will regrow if they're damaged.

A brief glimpse of this slender reptile slithering through low vegetation often leads to a moment of panic with the assumption that a snake is in the vicinity, but the distinctive shape of the head of the Burton's Snake-lizard is the initial clue to its true identity. It poses no threat to humans, but it's a different story for many species of lizards however, for from their perspective this is a beast from hell since it feeds almost exclusively on small reptiles.

Although it will hunt during the night, it's usually out and about during daylight hours when the creatures that are its prey are most active. Skinks, geckos, dragons and other legless lizards are the main ingredi-ents of a diet to which it occasionally adds small snakes, and it has an amazing physical characteristic that enables it to get a good grip on a meal. Its head has a unique flexi-ble hinged adaptation that allows the lizard, after grabbing its prey, to hold it firmly and to completely encircle its victim with its jaws. It's the only Australian lizard that has been gifted with this ability, and when it's suffocated its hapless prey, the Burton's Snake-lizard gulps it down head-first.

When females lay their eggs, they do so on the ground, usually among rocks, logs or leaf litter. They frequently lay more than one clutch of two eggs each year, and thus guarantee that this curious species will continue to wriggle across the Australian landscape.

This Carpet Python became aggressive when disturbed among some fallen palm fronds.

## CARPET PYTHON
*Morelia spilota*

The Carpet Python is found in many regions of northern, eastern and southern Australia, where its varied habitats include dry woodlands and forests, rainforests, coastal heathlands, farmlands, and urban parks and gardens.

This non-venomous snake, which can reach a length of 4m, has a highly variable range of colours and wears ornate patterns in a combination of hues, including cream, light and dark brown and black.

In the warm months of the year the Carpet Python is active both day and night as it hunts on the ground, in trees and shrubs, and in buildings for frogs, lizards, birds and mammals that it suffocates by wrapping itself around them with an unwelcome embrace before swallowing them whole. It visits poultry sheds where it's never averse to scoffing eggs, vulnerable chicks and adult birds, slithers through garden sheds and

Carpet Python dozing in a wheelbarrow.

These Carpet Python images were taken in the author's garden.

barns in search of rodents, and moves into houses too in search of any tasty morsels of food or a quiet and secluded place for an after-dinner nap.

In early summer, females seek out sheltered sites among bales of hay, in hollow logs, among rocks, or in discarded car tyres or heaps of other industrial or domestic rubbish, and settle down to the serious business of reproduction. Each coils herself around her clutch of eggs to keep them warm, and leaves only occasionally to soak up the warming sunlight to ensure that her body will provide the optimum temperature for the incubation of her eggs. The Carpet Python's maternal instinct stretches to nothing more than protecting her eggs from any threats by creatures that might regard them as a meal, and when the eggs hatch and the baby pythons wriggle out into the wild world, they're on their own, with their mother demonstrating no interest whatsoever in their well-being.

Many people see any snake as a threat, but the Carpet Python is one of the good guys of the reptilian world. It's generally non-aggressive and will usually slither slowly away if approached by a human, although it offers the benefits of its presence by controlling unwelcome vermin such as rats and mice, which do more damage to human interests than any Carpet Python could ever be accused of.

Red-bellied Black Snake at Bunnor Wetlands near Moree, New South Wales.

## RED-BELLIED BLACK SNAKE

*Pseudechis porphyriacus*

The Red-bellied Black Snake, which can be up to 2m in length, can be found in several separated regions of mainland Australia, including northern and central eastern Queensland, an area stretching from south-eastern Queensland and through eastern New South Wales and Victoria, and in South Australia's Mount Lofty Ranges. It's a species that's not particularly fussy about the type of habitat in which it resides, for it's as content among the vegetation on the banks of waterways, wetlands and farm dams as it is among that of forests, woodlands and grassy plains.

Although it can wriggle up into trees, this is a reptile that hunts on the ground, where its prey includes mammals, lizards, rodents and snakes. With cannibalistic tendencies, it has no reservations about eating members of its own species, and when a change of taste is the order of the day, the Red-bellied Black Snake takes to the water where, able to remain submerged for more than 20 minutes, it feasts on fish, frogs, tadpoles and yabbies.

As the warm weather of spring makes its welcome return, males are out and about searching for females that will ultimately give birth to 5–20 young that, in the earliest days of their lives, are vulnerable to attacks by predatory birds and reptiles, as well as by cats, foxes and dingoes. Although adults are threatened by few predators other than humans, there's one serious risk that they continue to face, and it's all to do with their diet. They're highly susceptible to the toxins contained within Cane Toads, and eating one of these introduced amphibians invariably results in the snake's death. It's the repugnant Cane Toad that's believed to be responsible for the considerable decline of populations of Red-bellied Black Snakes in the northern parts of this colourful reptile's range.

Despite the valuable role that it plays in the environment in controlling the numbers of other wild creatures and rodents, this is a venomous snake that most people would never want to see on their doorstep, but it's one of the most frequently encountered snakes on the eastern coast of Australia and is no stranger to urban areas. Fortunately, it's rarely aggressive, and will usually make a slithering retreat if anyone comes within its comfort zone, but if cornered or threatened, the Red-bellied Black Snake will vigorously defend itself and can give a painful and potentially fatal bite. Although several people are bitten every year, the number of fatalities is very low, with domestic cats and dogs and small children being the most likely to experience a negative outcome.

## KREFFT'S TURTLE
*Emydura macquarii krefftii*

The Krefft's Turtle – a subspecies of the Macquarie Turtle – is found in the wild only in Queensland. It inhabits rivers, wetlands and lakes on the eastern side of the Great Dividing Range, with its extensive

Krefft's Turtle beside a lake at Bundaberg Botanic Gardens, Queensland.

range stretching north from Brisbane to the Cape York Peninsula.

This short-necked turtle, which has a shell that's around 25cm long, is readily recognised by its distinctive pale yellow facial stripes that stretch from the rear of each eye to the ear-opening.

Thanks to the warm waters of its subtropical to tropical habitat, the Krefft's Turtle can remain active throughout the year, and it's often seen lazing on riverbank logs or rocks and in the calm waters of lakes in urban parks, from where it looks up, with a pleading stare, for the food that visitors invariably toss its way.

Juvenile Krefft's Turtles are carnivorous creatures that feed on aquatic insects, crustaceans and small fish, but as they mature they adopt a more varied diet with the addition of aquatic plants and fruits that have fallen into the water from overhanging trees.

In late spring and early summer, each mated female digs a nesting hollow well away from the water, lays her clutch of around 16 eggs, covers them with sand or soil and, leaving Mother Nature and fate to take care of the future, she waddles back to her aquatic home. The tiny hatchlings that eventually dig themselves out of the ground and make their way to the nearest source of water are little more than 25mm in length and are easy prey for fish, snakes and wading birds.

Turtles in a similar form to that of the Krefft's Turtle have meandered across the Earth's varied landscapes for some 200 million years, and although, particularly during times of drought, many of these dawdling reptiles are killed as they cross roads in search of a source of water, these fascinating creatures will undoubtedly remain members of the wildlife community that's on the doorstep of many Australians for generations to come.

Krefft's Turtle, with its shell cloaked with algae, in a lake at Tondoon Botanic Gardens in Gladstone, Queensland.

Double Drummer Cicada emerging from its shell during metamorphosis in the author's garden.

# INVERTEBRATES

## CENTIPEDE
*Scolopendramorpha* species

With this wriggling creature's common name stemming from the Latin prefix *centi*, meaning 'a hundred', and the word *pedis*, which means 'feet', it's a logical presumption that a centipede would have 100 feet, but that's not the case. Some have far more than 100, but the species illustrated here, which has a large head, a distinctive black stripe on each segment of its golden-brown body, and can grow to a length of 13cm, has one pair of feet for each of the 21 segments of its body, and a simple mathematical calculation reveals that it has a total of merely 42 feet.

The centipede is an ancient creature, with fossil records revealing that it evolved into its current form more than 400 million

The claws at the rear end of this centipede are used to hold its prey.

Centipede in the author's garden.

years ago when a gigantic species was more than a metre in length. Today an estimated 128 species of centipedes call Australia home. These curious creatures are part of a group known as chilopods, and are more closely related to shrimps, lobsters and crabs than they are to bugs and beetles.

Centipedes thrive in many diverse environments, with most preferring moist habitats, and they're often found under rocks and decaying logs or among the leaf litter on the floor of a forest or woodland.

This carnivorous character is a voracious predator that hunts its prey with skill and speed, generally at night. It feeds primarily on insects, earthworms and other small invertebrates that it grasps with the claws on the first section of its body, but these are not merely claws for restraining a struggling victim. They enable the centipede to bite and kill its prey with lethal venom, and that means that caution should be a priority whenever one of these creatures is around. They're not aggressive towards humans unless threatened, but their bite is something to be avoided, and although it will not prove fatal, a nip from a centipede is said to be excruciatingly painful.

Females each lay a clutch of around 60 eggs that they bury in the soil, and when these eventually hatch, a new brood of centipedes wriggles off to play their allotted and important role in the environment.

# INSECTS

Insects were the first creatures to fly through the skies more than 400 million years ago, and today there are twice as many species of insects in the world as there are all other animal species combined. Their population in merely 2 square kilometres of rural land exceeds that of the entire human population of the planet, and they owe their astounding success to a range of highly refined senses.

There are more than 62,000 identified species of insects in Australia, many of which are regarded as household, garden or agricultural pests, and although some, such as flies, mosquitoes and termites, are on no one's list of favourite creatures, all play an essential role in maintaining a healthy and balanced ecosystem, with many being food for larger creatures, and others being important pollinators or controlling populations of pest species.

Bugs and beetles, they're all the same many people may assume, but that's a far from correct assumption, for they belong to completely different groups of insects and have dramatically different lifestyles. Bugs have mouthparts that allow them to pierce their prey with a needle-sharp proboscis and suck up their body fluids, while beetles simply chew their food.

Some insects have unique chemoreceptors

Praying mantid in the author's garden.

on their mouthparts or, as with butterflies, on their feet to enable them to recognise the most desirable food plants, while others, including bees and wasps, utilise their highly sensitive antennae to locate food.

An insect's antennae are often erroneously referred to as 'feelers', but they allow insects to do more than simply touch the world around them, for they can also smell with their antennae and detect the flavours of the pollen or nectar of flowers, and of fruit, dung or decaying vegetation, and they also utilise their acute sense of smell to hunt their prey or to locate a mate.

Most predatory insects have additional receptors, minute hairs with extremely sensitive nerves at their base, which allow them to feel the slightest movements in the air around them and thus detect their prey, but for other species the main component of their success is their amazing eyesight.

Insects have compound eyes that are comprised of thousands of minute six-sided lenses that fit together like the cells of a honeycomb. This allows them to have an almost 360-degree view of their world and to detect and catch fast-flying insects that use speed as their primary weapon of defence. An astounding diversity of these amazing creatures can be discovered on the doorstep of everyone who's prepared to open their eyes and see that small is beautiful too.

# DOUBLE DRUMMER CICADA
*Thopha saccata*

This cicada's common name relates to the sound that it produces and that's created as it contracts a pair of ribbed membranes, known as timbals, which are on the sides of its abdomen, with the clicking sound that this action makes amplified in drum-like air-sacs in the abdomen. The resultant sound, which is used to attract a mate and that is reputedly the loudest noise created by any insect in the world, can reach a level of 100 decibels, which is the same level of noise as that produced by an angle grinder, a chainsaw or a personal stereo system that's turned up to full blast.

The Double Drummer, the largest of an estimated 800 species of Australian cicadas, is found in the forests and woodlands of much of eastern Australia, and in urban areas that have suitable trees for the continuation of the cicada's unusual lifestyle.

It's a lifecycle that no one could envy, for these curious insects spend the majority of their lives as nymphs that live underground where they feed on the sap of tree roots. The exact duration of the subterranean phase of their lives is unknown, but after several years, when they've finally reached maturity and the climatic conditions are right, they

Double Drummer Cicada after emerging from the ground.

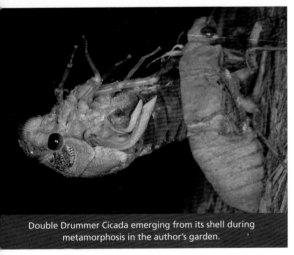

Double Drummer Cicada emerging from its shell during metamorphosis in the author's garden.

emerge from the darkness and climb onto the nearest tree trunk or stump to undergo their astounding transformation into winged adults.

The abandoned skins of the nymphs, which adorn tree trunks and fence posts during summer months, are conspicuous evidence that, from November to March, cicadas are on the move. The adults eventually fly up into the canopy of the trees where they spend the final 4–5 weeks of their lives. They feed on the sap of trees that they suck up using specialised mouthparts, and finally get down to the main reason for their arboreal existence, which is to produce the next generation of their species.

Shortly after mating, female cicadas settle down on a branch or on the trunk of a tree and lay their tiny eggs in a slit that they cut into the bark, and once their major role in life has been completed, the females die. When the eggs finally hatch, the nymphs tumble to the ground and burrow into the soil, and the weird and wonderful lifecycle of the cicada begins all over again.

Female Fiery Skimmer.

# DRAGONFLIES
Order Odonata

The dragonflies illustrated here are merely two of the more than 320 species that have been identified in Australia. The colourful Water Prince, *Hydrobasileus brevistylus*, is a large dragonfly in the hawker family which has a black and yellow spotted abdomen and a wingspan that is much longer than its body. The Fiery Skimmer, *Orthetrum villosovittatum*, which is also known as the 'bog skimmer', is an attractive insect too, with the female having a golden-brown body, and the vivid red male being an even more eye-catching creature.

Dragonflies existed long before dinosaurs strode across the world's diverse landscapes, with one species that lived around 250 million years ago and that had a wingspan of more than 70cm being the largest insect that has ever flown through the skies. The survival of dragonflies is primarily due to their large and highly developed eyes, the

Water Prince.

on a log or a branch with their wings spread out from the sides of their bodies, they're relatively easy to spot.

When a female dragonfly is ready to lay her eggs, she hovers above the water and repetitively dips the tip of her abdomen into the calm surface to release the eggs.

The larval and adult forms of many insect species differ dramatically in their appearance and lifestyles, and the variation between adults and their young is rarely more extreme than that demonstrated by dragonflies. The winged adults are masters of the skies, but their larvae are tiny aquatic creatures that feed on other aquatic animals, including the larvae of mosquitoes. The larvae themselves are often food for larger predators, such as fish, but those that survive and progress through approximately 12 larval stages eventually leave the water, and as their skins split open during the miracle of metamorphosis, the adult dragonflies emerge in all their glory.

Dragonfly larvae are extremely sensitive to water quality and require unpolluted water for their successful development and survival. The presence of a substantial population of dragonflies is an indication that all is well in the environment, but with some wetlands degraded, primarily by human activities, some species of these elegant creatures, which play an important role in controlling other insect populations, are teetering on the brink of extinction.

largest of any insect, and to their mastery of flight, for these graceful creatures, which can fly at up to 80km/h, are the aerial champions of the insect world, and have the ability not only to hover in mid-air, but also to make rapid sideways movements and to fly backwards. These skills enable them to be highly efficient predators, and as they hunt for flying insects, they stretch their front legs forward and effortlessly scoop up their prey in mid-air.

Dragonflies generally live in close proximity to a source of freshwater and, with males spending much of their time resting

Assassin bug nymph on a *Zinnia* flower.

## ASSASSIN BUG
*Pristhesancus plagipennis*

Assassin bugs are among the heroes of the insect world for they play a vital role in controlling populations of less welcome insect species, including those that cause serious damage to ornamental plants and to valuable agricultural crops. They'll feast on any insects that come within their reach, including grasshoppers, caterpillars and bees, and will also devour spiders.

Their common name relates to the fact that these stealthy predators silently approach an unsuspecting victim from behind and stab it with their powerful proboscis. They then inject their prey with an enzyme that liquefies the victim's internal organs, which the assassin bug can then suck up like a gruesome cocktail.

Each mature female lays a large number of eggs that eventually hatch to produce a swarm of tiny nymphs, which are around 5mm in length and appear, in the early stages of their lives, like a swarm of ants. The nymphs, which have bright orange and black bodies and legs and long antennae, pass through five phases of growth, which

Assassin bug. These images were taken in the author's garden.

are known as instars, before becoming adults. They bear a similar physical resemblance to adults, but are considerably smaller and don't have wings. At each stage of their transition to adulthood the colour of the nymphs intensifies and their size increases, and in the later stages they develop wing-buds, but with their wings not fully formed, flight is not an option for these young insects.

Adult assassin bugs have brown bodies, the same long legs and antennae that are conspicuous features of nymphs, and transparent wings that allow them to enjoy the freedom of the skies.

With their great appetite for insects, these are creatures that are welcome in any garden or agricultural area, and they're most active and thus easier to see in summer months when there's an increase in the population of the insects on which they feed.

These savage little assassins are not aggressive towards humans, but should be treated with caution and respect, for they may attack when threatened, and when they bite the fingers of a hand that comes too close for comfort, they inject the same substance that they use to convert the innards of each victim into a tasty soup. Such a bite, although not fatal, can be very painful indeed, if those who are unfortunate enough to have experienced it are to be believed.

Hairy Flower Wasp on a rose bud.

## HAIRY FLOWER WASP
*Campsomeris tasmaniensis*

Anyone who thinks that the words 'wasp' and 'sting' are synonymous, and who has a fear of all wasps, should reassess their concerns. Some, including the aptly named Hairy Flower Wasp, are among the most beneficial of all insect species.

They can be found in most regions of Australia, and while their natural habitat, prior to the arrival of Europeans, was in native woodlands and forests, they're now regular residents in urban parks and gardens, and every gardener should be thrilled to see them.

Hairy Flower Wasps, which have orange to yellow bodies with black stripes, and opaque yellowish-brown wings, are solitary creatures that, unlike many other species of wasps, do not make a nest or live in colonies. They have the ability to sting, but with no nest or colony to defend they have no need for aggression, and thus pose no threat to humans.

They feed on the energy-rich nectar of flowers, and as the dense covering of hairs on their bodies becomes dusted with golden pollen, these large wasps play a valuable role as pollinators as they move from one delicate bloom to another.

Humans certainly have no reason to fear the Hairy Flower Wasp, but if beetles were aware of what the future had in store for them they'd be quaking in terror the moment one of these winged creatures fluttered onto the scene. When ready to lay her eggs, the female searches for the fat and juicy larvae of beetles, such as Rhinoceros and Christmas Beetles that are often found in farmyard manure, in a garden compost heap, or in rotting wood, and she also hunts for grubs that thrive in the soil of sugar cane plantations. When she's located her victim, the wasp stings it, lays an egg in its fleshy body, and buries her victim in the ground or in the rotting wood where she discovered it, leaving it to die a slow and lingering death. The wasp's sting merely paralyses her victim, and as the egg laid within it hatches, the emerging larva feasts on living flesh.

Nature has endowed some insect species with savage techniques with which to ensure the survival of their offspring, but the gruesome reproductive methods of the Hairy Flower Wasp ensure that, by effectively controlling populations of other insect species, this tiny creature is one of Mother Nature's most invaluable little helpers.

## YELLOW-BROWN PAPER WASP
*Ropalidia romandi*

The Yellow-brown Paper Wasp, which is found in northern and eastern regions of the Australian mainland, is an insect that

Yellow-brown Paper Wasp on a flower.

many people have been introduced to in a way that they'd rather forget, for despite the fact that it's only about 12mm in length, this colourful little creature can inflict a very painful sting.

These relatively common wasps are highly social insects that live in colonies within nests that are created from a tough material that the wasps make by chewing bits of decaying wood and blending it with their saliva. Their nests, which consist of numerous individual cells enclosed within a paper-like covering, are often attached to the underside of the branch of a tree, and at times they hang from a wire fence or are suspended under the eaves of a building.

The colony's queen dutifully lays an egg in each cell within the nest, and when the larvae eventually hatch, they're fed with pre-digested caterpillars that other members of the colony have laboriously collected. When the larvae are fully grown, the diligent workers of the group seal them into their individual cells where they pupate and finally emerge as adult wasps, and thus expand the colony.

In hot summer months adult wasps congregate on the edges of garden bird baths and pools or on the muddy banks of streams to sip at the water, and they dine on the nectar of flowers. In winter, when their favoured food may be in short supply, they occasionally feed on the honeydew secreted by scale insects.

Yellow-brown Paper Wasps are important members of the wildlife community, for they offer gardeners and farmers a helping hand in the ongoing battle to control ravenous caterpillars. They're best left alone to go about their lives unhindered, unless they've built their nest a little too close to the doorstep of a house, for although they rarely sting, other than when aggressively defending their nest from a perceived threat, a close encounter with one of these tiny creatures is not the most pleasurable of experiences.

## BLOWFLY
*Calliphora* species

Blowflies are unlikely to be on anyone's list of beautiful wild creatures, but despite the fact that most people would rather kill them than take a moment to look at them in detail, they're fascinating insects that have an important function within a balanced ecosystem.

These are the familiar flies that are seen, often in large numbers, around rubbish bins, animal faeces, and rotting meat or carcasses. It's probably no surprise to hear that insects that feed and dabble about in such revolting places are implicated in the spread of diseases.

The blowfly, which is larger than a common housefly is, on close inspection, a surprisingly attractive creature, with several species having spectacular and gleaming metallic blue-green colouration, and it's this that gives the fly its other colloquial name of 'bluebottle'.

The blowfly's reddish-brown eyes are its most amazing feature however, for like all flies, it has large compound eyes that are made up of thousands of tiny eyes that enable it to have an astounding range of vision and an almost 360-degree view of the world around it. That's why, when you try to stalk one from behind with a fly swatter at the ready, it sees you coming and takes evasive action.

Blowflies live anywhere where they can find the putrid and decomposing stuff on which they feed. The search for all things with a foul smell often leads them to plants, such as succulent stapelias, that emit an odour like rotting flesh. Grains of pollen adhere to the hairs on the bodies of visiting

*Calliphora* blowfly in the author's garden.

flies, and as they move from one flower to another, they do the plants a favour by pollinating them. Blowflies are also lured to several species of fungi, such as the decorative stinkhorns that also have a pungent odour, and the flies unwittingly become carriers of minute spores and give the fungi some assistance in colonising new areas.

Other aspects of the blowfly's lifestyle are far less pleasant, including the fact that the female, after mating, lays her eggs in the same place where she has been feeding, usually in the decomposing flesh of a dead animal. The white larvae, known as maggots, which eventually emerge from the eggs, are born with a ravenous appetite and tear at the stinking flesh of their nursery, with ingredients of their saliva able to soften their food so that it can easily be digested. After around 10 days of feasting, the larvae burrow into the nearby soil where they pupate in cocoons, from which another generation of blowflies will eventually emerge.

Although most people despise these wild creatures that are on everyone's doorstep at some time or another, blowflies justify their existence by working tirelessly to clean up nature's detritus of birds and animals that have come to the end of their relatively brief lives, and they themselves provide a nutritious source of food for the many creatures, including the birds, frogs and reptiles with which they share their environment.

# HOVERFLY
*Episyrphus* species

There are few people other than entomologists who can honestly say that they like flies, but although some are unwelcome creatures that spread diseases, others are particularly valuable members of the community of insects that reside within a garden or agricultural environment, and the hoverfly is definitely one of the heroes of the insect world.

It's easy to mistake this colourful fly for a wasp, and that's its intention, but although its appearance mimics that of a wasp, its huge eyes are the most conspicuous clue to its true identity. Like all flies it has compound eyes that are comprised of many thousands of individual lenses and that give flies the ability to see light and colours that are invisible to the human eye, and also enable them to see fast moving small objects, such as other insects.

The hoverfly has small and inconspicuous antennae, transparent wings, a slender orange body with black stripes and a waist that's narrow like that of a wasp. However, gaudy hoverflies, which are found throughout Australia, and are most commonly seen in the warmer months of the year, do not sting and are quite harmless, at least to humans.

They frequently hover in the air and

Hoverfly on a flower.

descend to feed on the nectar of flowers, and with pollen dusting their bodies, they're valuable pollinators of many species of plants. There's another reason why these attractive insects are always welcome in a garden. They usually lay their eggs on leaves that are close to a colony of aphids, and the tiny larvae that eventually hatch play a vital role in controlling garden pests, for they are voracious predators that feed primarily on aphids, and also on other unwelcome insects such as scale insects and thrips.

## PRAYING MANTID

Order Mantodea

There are approximately 200 species of praying mantids in Australia, the majority of which live in subtropical and tropical regions, and there's perennial confusion regarding the common name of these fascinating insects. 'Praying mantid' is the most frequently used name, as the insect's stance, in the opinion of those with some imagination, resembles that of a person praying, while 'preying mantid' is an equally appropriate name for this skilful predator that preys on a wide range of other insects.

A praying mantid has a long slender body that's either brown or green, a triangular head that can swivel round for almost 360 degrees, large and prominent eyes, long thin antennae and long legs with rows of savage spines on the forelegs. Its wings lie flat on its body when not in use, and although males can fly, the females of some species

These praying mantid images were taken in the author's garden.

either have smaller wings that provide only a limited ability to fly or have no wings at all. Females are usually considerably larger than males, but despite their often relatively large size, they can be difficult to discover in their natural habitat where they are well camouflaged and frequently resemble twigs or leaves.

A praying mantid, in its iconic pose and waiting patiently among vegetation, may appear to be appealing for a potential victim to wander its way, and when its prayers are answered it attacks with astounding speed, grabs its prey with its powerful forelegs, and quickly devours it.

When these curious insects themselves are threatened, speed is not a factor in their survival technique, for although most can fly, they do so only rather slowly and awkwardly. They are the favoured prey of many other predators and rely heavily on their camouflage to avoid becoming a snack for a hungry bird or reptile.

They're usually solitary creatures that come together only when mating, and making the acquaintance of a female is bad news for a male, for the female has a reputation for eating her suitor after mating – a fact that's true for some species that have cannibalistic tendencies. Females lay their

Praying mantids in the author's garden.

eggs in a spongy case called an ootheca, which is usually attached to the branch of a tree or to foliage. Large numbers of tiny mantids eventually hatch and set off into the wide world where they, like their parents, will play a valuable role in the natural environment, in farmlands and in gardens as the welcome predators that control many insect pests.

## RHINOCEROS BEETLE

*Xylotrupes ulysses*

The Rhinoceros Beetle, which is also often referred to as an 'elephant beetle', is the largest of all the beetles found in Australia. It inhabits warm and humid subtropical and tropical regions of the continent, primarily in Queensland, the Northern Territory and northern New South Wales, and is also found in South-East Asia and Indonesia.

Like many flying insects, it's attracted to lights and is often seen under suburban street lights, but the other place where it's regularly found is on or close to the sprawling poinciana trees that are widely grown in streets, parklands and gardens within the beetle's extensive range.

The Rhinoceros Beetle, which can measure up to 50mm in length, is completely black, and males are easily recognised by the large and distinctive horns that are their primary weapons in seasonal battles for a mate. When disturbed, they make an agitated hissing noise by rubbing their wing covers against their abdomen, and although this may sound threatening, these giants of the insect world pose no danger to humans.

Adults feed on the leaves, soft bark and new shoots of trees, with large populations gathering on a tree when they're ready to mate. Each female emits a pheromone that attracts a group of males that, all eager for her attentions, engage in vigorous combat, with the strongest using its horns to push its weaker rivals from the tree.

Villagers in Thailand, where Rhinoceros Beetles are also common, have taken advantage of the insect's fighting instincts to indulge their passion for gambling. After a female beetle has been sealed inside a bamboo tube, males are placed on the outside and the owners of individual beetles place their bets on which insect will push the other off the bamboo in a game that's only a minor improvement on betting on two flies climbing up a wall.

Female beetles lay their eggs in decomposing vegetable matter on which the newly hatched larvae feed. These fat white grubs are often found in heaps of compost, and when they're ready to begin the next phase of their lifecycle, they pupate in the soil, and after metamorphosis a new Rhinoceros Beetle emerges, digs its way out of the ground, and heads to the nearest poinciana tree or another favoured plant.

They cause minimal damage to trees and, thanks to their hard shells and horns, are not the preferred prey of many other creatures. The larvae, which play a useful role in breaking down decaying plant material, are more vulnerable, and are a major source of food for many species of birds, including kookaburras and magpies that will snatch them from the soil the moment they dare to peer above the surface.

Rhinoceros Beetle in the author's garden.

Blue Triangle butterflies mating.

# BUTTERFLIES, MOTHS AND CATERPILLARS

**A**ustralia is home to approximately 400 identified species of butterflies and an estimated 10,000 species of moths. Many feed on the nectar produced by flowers or on the juices of decaying fruit. Some delicately sip moisture from wet sand or mud beside waterways and pools, but others survive, for the entirety of their relatively short lives, on nothing more than the reserves that they stored in their bodies during the phase of their lives in which they were caterpillars.

It's sex, rather than food, that dominates the lives of adult butterflies and moths, and they don't rely entirely on their good looks to attract a mate. Female moths produce pheromones that have an odour that's readily detected by males, and when a male flutters close to a female, the pheromones that he too emits are enough to persuade her to mate with him. Butterflies also produce pheromones to attract prospective mates, but only males have this ability.

After mating, which often occurs while both partners are in flight, a female butterfly or moth has an important decision to make. She has to choose the right plant on which to lay her eggs, for her larvae, the tiny caterpillars that will eventually hatch from the eggs, are extremely fastidious and will only feed on very specific plant species. Using highly sensitive receptors in her antennae, her legs and the tip of her abdomen, each female 'tastes' the foliage to ensure that it will be a suitable food plant for her caterpillars, and when satisfied that she's made the appropriate choice, she silently deposits her eggs.

Some of the plants utilised by butterflies and moths contain toxins that would prove harmful, even fatal, to humans who might consume the foliage, but they have no detrimental effects on the caterpillars that devour them. Some, on the contrary, gain positive benefits from plant toxins that they store in their bodies to be used as chemical weapons, which are merely one of the varied defence strategies that caterpillars employ to deter predators.

Caterpillar of Four-spotted Cup Moth.

Blue Triangle on a daylily flower, soon to become the prey of a waiting flower spider.

## BLUE TRIANGLE

*Graphium sarpedon*

The Blue Triangle, which is one of the most beautiful and easily recognisable of all Australian butterflies, can be spotted fluttering silently through the air in eastern Australia, from Cape York in Queensland to southern New South Wales. Although its favoured habitat is among damp forests and woodlands, it's also commonly seen in urban parks and gardens.

Its wings are black to dark brown with a large vivid blue triangular area dominating each wing, and the pattern on the underside of its wings is similar, with the exception of a few bright red spots near the top and bottom edges of the wings.

The caterpillar of the Blue Triangle is a far less attractive character, for its bright green body is decorated with nothing more than a white stripe near the head.

When disturbed or threatened the caterpillar brings out its most potent weapon, which comes in the form of a yellow horn-shaped feature, known as an osmeterium, that emerges from behind the caterpillar's head. The strong and unpleasant odour that it emits is enough to keep all but the most determined of predators at bay, and anyone in the vicinity of one of these wriggling creatures is likely to smell it well before they see it, for this is a caterpillar that's well camouflaged among the verdant foliage on which it feeds.

# MEADOW ARGUS
*Junonia villida*

Meadow Argus feeding on the flowers of a melaleuca tree near Taroom, Queensland.

With the Meadow Argus found throughout Australia, no one needs the luck of a lottery winner to catch a glimpse of this spectacular creature, for although it's at home in forests and woodlands, it will also flutter through any urban areas where suitable food is available.

Like most butterflies, it feeds on the nectar of flowers, but its caterpillars are not so particular about what they eat, for a wide range of foliage, including that of introduced garden plants and many species of invasive weeds, is on their daily menu.

The spiny black caterpillars of the Meadow Argus are not the most attractive of insects, but thanks to the miracle of metamorphosis they eventually abandon their drab attire and don regal garb as they become winged creatures that draw a gasp of wonder from all who see them. This is a butterfly with a brown hairy body, and with wings that have both brown and vivid orange patches, and dark and light brown stripes at their edges. The most prominent feature of the Meadow Argus butterfly however, is the array of large dark blue to black eye-spots on each of its wings. Although they add to its beauty, their main purpose is to fool predators that might view this fragile creature as an easy meal.

They bite at the butterfly's false 'eyes' and, although an attack may damage its wings, the butterfly's body remains unharmed and it survives to fly another day.

During October and November Meadow Argus butterflies usually abandon southern areas and flutter north where they gather in large numbers, often in the company of Australian Painted Lady butterflies, and sip on the nectar of flowers, with those of melaleuca trees proving irresistible. Their lifecycle, through the varied stages of egg, caterpillar, pupa and butterfly, lasts a mere 53 days, but these are creatures that, in the final adult phase of their lives, leave a lasting memory of the wonders of nature on all who are privileged to see them.

Wanderer butterfly.

# WANDERER

*Danaus plexippus*

**W**anderers are famous for their seasonal migrations during which they travel vast distances across North America and congregate in populations of many hundreds of thousands. It was in the 19th century that these beautiful creatures, which are also known as Monarch or Milkweed butterflies, completed what must have been one of their greatest journeys as they crossed the Pacific Ocean to Australia, with the first sighting here being in the summer of 1871.

It's a trek that these colourful butterflies, which have vivid orange wings with prominent black veins and black borders freckled with white spots, might have been

undertaking for millennia, but it was only after Europeans arrived in Australia and introduced a range of exotic plants to the continent that Wanderers could finally make themselves at home down under.

When female Wanderers discovered the plants that their larvae would need for food, they laid their eggs and the first caterpillars of this exotic species eventually crept onto the scene – their bodies adorned with yellow, black and white bands. Today they're a relatively common sight in eastern coastal regions, and are occasionally found in Victoria and eastern South Australia.

The most important plant in the Wanderer's lifecycle, the species on which females lay their eggs and on which ravenous caterpillars feast, is *Asclepias curassavica*,

Wanderer butterfly.

a plant that's commonly referred to as 'tropical milkweed', and that had its origins in North America. With its clusters of vivid red and orange flowers, it's a weed that's not out of place in a garden designed to attract butterflies but, in common with other species of milkweeds, it has a hidden secret. Its white sap is poisonous, but the caterpillars that nibble on its foliage are unaffected by its toxins and use them to their own advantage. With the plant's poison in their system, both the caterpillars and the butterflies that they finally become are poisonous to most predatory birds. Mother Nature ensures that the wild creatures of Australia continually evolve and adapt to the changing world around them, and some birds, including Pied Currawongs and Black-faced Cuckooshrikes, occasionally scoff the caterpillars with no ill effects.

The caterpillar of a Saunders' Case Moth emerging from its woven retreat.

# SAUNDERS' CASE MOTH
*Metura elongatus*

The Saunders' Case Moth, which is found in eastern Australia, including Tasmania, has a very unconventional way of life and a unique method of protecting itself from potential predators. It's the curious home of the moth's caterpillar that's most frequently seen, and anyone with a little patience might be treated to a glimpse of the bright orange and black caterpillar as it peers cautiously from the doorway of its camouflaged retreat. After creating a cylindrical silken sac that's covered with fragments of leaves, this ingenious caterpillar then adds a layer of twigs to create a mobile home that it carries with it as it moves around like a hermit crab in a recycled ocean shell.

The Saunders' Case Moth caterpillar feeds on the foliage of a wide range of native plants, in addition to several exotic species. With its head and part of its body protruding from its case, it also feeds on the grasses of lawns, but will retreat to the safety of its home the moment it feels threatened.

Each caterpillar remains in its case for 1–2 years, and when it's ready to pupate, it attaches the open end of its case to the trunk or branch of a tree or to the wall of a building, positions itself head-downwards, and waits for the miracle of metamorphosis to take place.

When a small male moth, with black wings, an orange furry head, and a black and orange striped furry body, finally emerges, he flies off in search of a mate. Females, which have no wings, remain in the case for the entirety of their lives and, after mating, they lay their eggs within the security of their well-camouflaged home. When the eggs ultimately hatch, the tiny caterpillars emerge from a hole at the rear of the case, and lower themselves, via silken threads, onto the nearest branch or foliage where each begins to create its own retreat that it will continually enlarge as it grows.

When additional space is required, the caterpillar, using its strong jaws, snips off a fragment of a twig that it attaches to the mouth of the case with a strand of silk. It then pulls its head back inside the case and slowly cuts a slot through the tough silken wall. This tiny construction worker then pokes its head out through the hole, grabs the newly cut piece of twig, severs the silk that held it in place, pulls the twig over the hole, and secures it firmly to the body of the case. With this one task taking more than an hour to complete, the construction of an entire case, which can be up to 10cm long, is no mean feat for the Saunders' Case Moth caterpillar.

## TAILED EMPEROR
*Polyura sempronius*

Although the Tailed Emperor butterfly prefers to live in subtropical and tropical regions it can also be found in areas with cooler climates, although it never ventures as far south as Tasmania. It's not the most colourful of butterflies, but with wings that are predominantly black and creamy-white on the upperside and that have pointed 'tails', it's still an attractive creature that can be seen feeding on flowers or on the juices of decaying fruit.

When it comes to glamour, the caterpillar of the Tailed Emperor is in a different league altogether, for it's a creature that some people may find repulsive. In its earliest stages, it's a yellowish-brown colour with a black head, but as it grows it becomes emerald green and develops a succession of wide yellow bands around its body and a narrow yellow stripe along the lower section of each side. Its most curious physical feature is the strange shield and the array of yellow-edged green horns that rise from

Close-up of the caterpillar of the Tailed Emperor.

its head, and this strange caterpillar gives its presence away by emitting a foul smell whenever it considers that danger is on the doorstep.

It's a far from fussy creature when food is on its tiny mind, and will gorge itself on the foliage of many native and exotic plants including cordylines, acacia, poinciana and camphor laurel trees.

Caterpillar of a Tailed Emperor.

# LILY BORER
*Brithys crini*

Few people would give the inconspicuous brown Lily Borer moth a second glance, for it's a small and drab creature that flutters silently through the night, but its caterpillars are impossible to ignore. Found in the Northern Territory, Queensland and New South Wales, they have black bodies ringed by white spots, and orange to brown heads and rear-ends, but it's the damage they cause to plants, rather than their physical appearance, that draws both the attention and the ire of gardeners.

The female moths lay clusters of eggs on the foliage of host plants and the tiny caterpillars that eventually emerge begin a feeding frenzy. It's plants within the lily family, including Crinum Lilies, hippeastrums and Rain Lilies, that come under sustained attack.

Some caterpillars bore into the stems of the plant's large and fleshy leaves, while others feast on the leaves themselves, eating the most succulent parts and remaining beneath the leaf's translucent outer layer, its epidermis. As the onslaught progresses, every leaf turns a sickly yellow, the stems wilt, and the plant appears to be in its death throes, but with the caterpillars' food plants being bulbous species, they survive the rampaging hordes and live to flower another day.

Each caterpillar is believed to consume around 2.4 square metres of plant material during its brief lifetime, and with their insatiable appetites for plants that contain toxins, the caterpillars are unpalatable to most predators, and that means that gardeners can expect little if any help from Mother Nature in their attempts to limit the damage caused by these unwelcome visitors.

## CUP MOTHS
*Doratifera* species

Cup moths are small, often brown and rather unimpressive creatures, but the same can't be said about their larvae, which are among the most brightly coloured and unusual of all caterpillars. They're also among the most dangerous, as botanist Joseph Banks discovered during his adventurous journey with Captain James Cook in 1770. He was the first to record the presence of cup moths in Australia, and had the dubious honour of being the first non-indigenous person to be stung by a cup moth caterpillar. The sting, according to others who have shared his experience, is not something to be forgotten in a hurry.

The bodies of the caterpillars of most species of cup moths have numerous short spines, each of which are hollow and

Lily Borer caterpillar feeding on a leaf.

Caterpillar of Four-spotted Cup Moth.

contain venom. When an unwary human or predator touches the needle-sharp spines, the tips break and the venom is injected into the flesh.

Cup moths owe their collective name to the cup-shaped cocoons that their caterpillars create when preparing to pupate, and that are usually attached to the twigs of the caterpillars' food plants, which include eucalyptus, melaleuca and acacia trees.

Cup moth caterpillars are often referred to as 'slug caterpillars' due to the fact that, with some of their legs having evolved to become little more than suckers, they move along with a motion similar to that of slugs, with the aid of a type of liquefied silk that allows them to slide effortlessly across the rough surfaces of twigs and branches.

Females, after laying their eggs on the leaves of the plants that will provide their larvae with food, cover the eggs with hairs from their bodies. This camouflage improves the chances that the eggs will survive, but the caterpillars that eventually hatch are not always so lucky, for despite their savage armoury of spines, many come under attack by birds and by parasitic insects that lay their eggs in the soft flesh of the caterpillars' bodies.

The species illustrated are the Four-spotted Cup Moth, *Doratifera quadriguttata*, which is found in all states other than Western Australia, and the Mottled Cup Moth, *Doratifera vulnerans*, which is found only in eastern coastal regions of the continent. The caterpillars of both species feed on the leaves of mangrove trees and several species of fruit trees, in addition to those of their favoured indigenous plants. Despite their ornate patterns, they're surprisingly well camouflaged in their natural habitat.

The Four-spotted Cup Moth's caterpillar, with its rows of fleshy spines, looks convincingly threatening, but the caterpillar of the Mottled Cup Moth often appears completely harmless, for it retracts its red spines and gives no hint of the weapons that it has at its disposal. It's a different matter when it feels threatened however, for an array of ferocious spines suddenly appears as the caterpillar reinforces the message that it's neither a creature that will make a tasty snack for a predator, nor one that should be handled carelessly be humans. Anyone who fails to heed that message is sure to regret the fact that Mother Nature's visual warning to look but not touch was ignored.

Caterpillar of Mottled Cup Moth. Both images were taken in the author's garden.

White flower spider on a *Nemesia* flower.

# SPIDERS

**M**any people have an innate fear of spiders, yet these are the environment's unsung heroes without which the world as we know it would not exist. That might sound like an exaggeration, but British researchers have estimated that spiders consume some 120kg of insects per hectare daily. Without them, or with their numbers significantly reduced, there would be a massive escalation of the insect population resulting in the widespread destruction of crops, which would inevitably lead to famine and starvation on a global scale.

From their origins 360 million years ago, spiders have evolved in ways that enable them to survive in almost every environment on Earth, from coastal rock pools, caves, swamps and forests, to deserts and snow-capped mountains. The crowning glory of their evolutionary progress was the ability to produce silk, and it's this amazing feature and their ingenious use of what is reputedly the world's strongest natural fibre that has enabled spiders to become highly efficient predators.

More than a third of the approximately 2,000 species of spiders that call Australia home are web-builders, others create sticky traps to capture their prey, and many are hunters that chase and pounce upon their victims with lightning speed. With most spiders having at least eight eyes and the ability to see in all directions simultaneously, escape is rarely an option for any insect that comes within a spider's gaze.

Fortunately, only a few Australian spiders are capable of inflicting a bite that may cause significant pain or prove fatal to humans. The toxin of the daddy long-legs is the most potent of any species, but its fangs are too small to bite humans. The Sydney Funnel-web, which has occasionally caused fatalities, the mouse spiders, the Australian Redback, which can inflict a painful although rarely lethal bite, and wolf and white-tailed spiders that are suspected of causing slow-healing skin sores are undoubtedly creatures to be avoided, but most spiders should be considered as beneficial members of the wildlife community, and not an enemy that should be eradicated.

## GREEN HUNTSMAN SPIDER
*Neosparassus* species

**T**he green huntsman spider, which hides under the loose bark of trees, in crevices among rocks, and on foliage, catches its prey by waiting in ambush for a prospective victim to pass by, rather than by constructing a web, and with its two front pairs of legs considerably longer than those at the rear of its body it's well designed to be an efficient predator.

The female creates a silken egg-sac and guards it until the newly hatched spiderlings emerge. Like any caring mother, she'll attempt to defend her young from danger and may become aggressive if approached while watching over her eggs, and with her bite causing humans severe pain, as well as nausea and vomiting, she's not a creature that should be provoked.

With *Neosparassus* species found throughout the continent, there's a good chance that one of these well-camouflaged spiders could be right on the doorstep of millions of Australians.

# HUNTSMAN SPIDER
*Heteropoda* species

It's extremely difficult to distinguish one *Heteropoda* species of spider from another, but all are known as 'huntsman spiders' and are found in most regions of Australia. As their common name suggests, these large predominantly brown spiders are free hunters rather than web-builders, and will wander into any environment that's inhabited by the tiny creatures on which they feed.

This green huntsman spider had been hiding in a bromeliad in the author's garden and emerged when the plant was watered.

*Heteropoda* huntsman spider camouflaged on the bark of a gum tree.

They're most active at night when they hunt for their prey, and their lightning-fast speed, together with the effective camouflage of their mottled brown or grey colouration are the major factors in their success as formidable predators.

They're not too fastidious when it comes to food, and a wide range of insects and other invertebrates are on their menu, and that means that these often very large spiders, which may have a leg span of up to 15cm, should be admired more than despised, for they play an invaluable role in controlling the populations of many unwelcome insects with which they share a great diversity of habitats.

Many huntsman spiders have flattened bodies that enable them to crawl under loose bark and into narrow crevices among rocks and brickwork, and legs that, instead of bending downwards in relation to the spider's body, have joints that enable the legs to stretch forward and laterally in a crab-like fashion.

Female *Heteropoda* huntsman spider with egg-sac on the side of a flowerpot outside author's house.

After mating, a female huntsman spider creates a flat, white silken egg-sac in which she lays around 200 eggs. She places it in a concealed location, which may be under the bark of a tree, on the side of a plant pot in a dark and shaded corner of a fernery, or even behind the curtain in a house, and settles down to her maternal duties. She guards her egg-sac, without taking any respite to eat, for around three weeks, and it's when the tiny spiderlings hatch and crawl from their nursery that some species of huntsman

spiders provide an astounding demonstration of their strong maternal instinct.

A doting mother will often feed her young with a regurgitated slurry of her prey, and, if they're threatened, even by a human momentarily moving too close for comfort, she'll raise herself up on her long legs to enable her vast brood to shelter beneath her huge body, like a mother hen protecting her chicks. She devotedly guards her spiderlings for several weeks until the time comes for each of them to set off on its own adventure into the world beyond the security of its nursery.

Young spiders, like their parents, are an important source of food for birds, reptiles and predatory wasps, and humans who have no hesitation in eradicating a spider by stomping on it or obliterating it with a blast of poison from a can of insecticide are also their enemy. Anyone who suffers from arachnophobia can be forgiven for their fear of these gargantuan arachnids, but other members of the human race have no justifiable reason to fear these spiders that, in the scheme of things, are definitely friend not foe.

It's an undeniable fact that some huntsman spiders will bite if threatened, and the results, although not fatal, can include unpleasant symptoms, such as sweating, nausea and even vomiting, and that's one very good reason to treat these amazing creatures with great respect.

Giant Grey Huntsman spider in the author's garden.

# GIANT GREY HUNTSMAN

*Holconia immanis*

Large and hairy spiders can be the stuff of nightmares, and the mere thought of a close encounter with this spider, one of the largest huntsman spiders in Australia, is enough to make many people tremble in their shoes. The Giant Grey Huntsman, which is found only in eastern Australia, from Queensland to Victoria, has a body length of around 5cm and legs that, when outstretched, are some 17cm across, and although it can give a painful bite if provoked, there's no genuine reason to fear this imposing creature.

With its relatively flattened body, it can hide under loose bark, or shelter among the leaf litter on a forest floor or the mulch of a garden bed, and it makes itself at home in the dark corners of sheds and occasionally in houses.

With its grey to brown hairy body and legs, a dark brown to black streak on its abdomen and eight eyes in two rows of four, the Giant Grey Huntsman is very distinctive, and although it generally searches for its prey under cover of darkness, it's often seen out and about during the day or discovered in some secluded retreat as it waits silently for a prospective victim to dawdle past.

The female devotedly guards her silken egg-sac and protects her myriads of tiny spiderlings until the day arrives when, at the whims of a subtle breeze and with the aid of threads of silk that act as delicate parachutes, they're carried across the landscape to begin their lives in a world where insects, the good, the bad, and the decidedly ugly, vastly outnumber the human species.

Yellow flower spider with its prey – a bee that had been visiting flowers near the spider's lair.

## FLOWER SPIDER

*Thomisus spectabilis*

This flower spider, which is found throughout Australia and is particularly common in eastern regions, is also known as a 'crab spider' – a name it owes to the fact that its front legs, with which its grabs its prey, are usually held in a position similar to that of a crab.

Females, which can vary in colour from white to yellow, are far larger and more conspicuous than males, which are usually brown, and although they rely on camouflage to catch their prey, it's their almost limitless patience that ultimately brings results, but they don't spend their days and nights waiting for their prey to fly into a sticky web.

White spiders may conceal themselves

White flower spider – the images of this species were taken in the author's garden.

on the petals of a white flower, and yellow spiders often choose a yellow bloom as their hunting ground, but on many occasions the idea of camouflage, at least as seen by human eyes, seems to have been thrown out of the window, for vivid pink or red flowers are among the flower spider's favoured haunts.

Bees, butterflies and other insects that visit flowers are this spider's primary prey, and with an individual spending several days on the same flower, its patience ultimately pays off as an unsuspecting victim eventually wanders within reach.

When it's time to start a family, the female creates a silken egg-sac, usually on the underside of a leaf, and guards it until the minute spiderlings eventually hatch and make their way onto nearby flowers to begin their lives alone.

The bite of a flower spider signals instant death for its insect victim, and although the bite of one of these attractive little spiders has no serious consequences for any human that feels its wrath, it can cause considerable short-term pain. Fortunately, the spider's instinctive reaction when a human comes within its field of vision is to scurry away, and that means that there's almost as much chance of being bitten by one of these diminutive predators as there is of being whisked away to foreign lands on a magical flying carpet.

Male on rose leaf.

## NORTHERN GREEN JUMPING SPIDER

*Mopsus mormon*

Beauty, someone once insisted, is all in the eye of the beholder, and with this spider's species name *mormon* being a derivative of an ancient Greek word describing a 'she-monster' or 'hobgoblin', the taxonomist who gave this wild creature its scientific name obviously didn't see it as an attractive creature. The origins of the name of its genus are far less clear however, for *Mopsus* was a mythological Greek hero who was the son of Apollo and a revered seer who could understand the speech of birds, a talent that, as yet, is not known to be one shared by the Northern Green Jumping Spider.

This highly distinctive spider is among the largest of Australia's many species of jumping spiders, but being merely 1.5cm long, it's certainly not a beast of gargantuan proportions. It's found in Queensland, northern New South Wales, the Northern Territory and Western Australia, and although it inhabits woodlands and forests, it's equally at home in urban parks and gardens.

Like many spiders, it's a master of camouflage, and with its vivid green colouration it's often hard to see when it's hunting for its prey among verdant foliage. The most conspicuous physical characteristics of the female of this species are its variable but generally leaf-green colour, the distinctive brown and white pattern on its face, and the two black lines along its teardrop-shaped abdomen, while the male has a prominent moustache of white hairs on each side of its face.

The Northern Green Jumping Spider, rather than build a web to catch its prey, simply leaps, with incredible agility, onto its victim and kills it with a bite that injects venom. Although the doomed creature rapidly succumbs to the effects of the poison, humans who are unfortunate enough to be bitten by this strange little spider will suffer no more than a brief period of localised pain.

Female Northern Green Jumping Spider on a bromeliad leaf. The images of this species were taken in the author's garden.

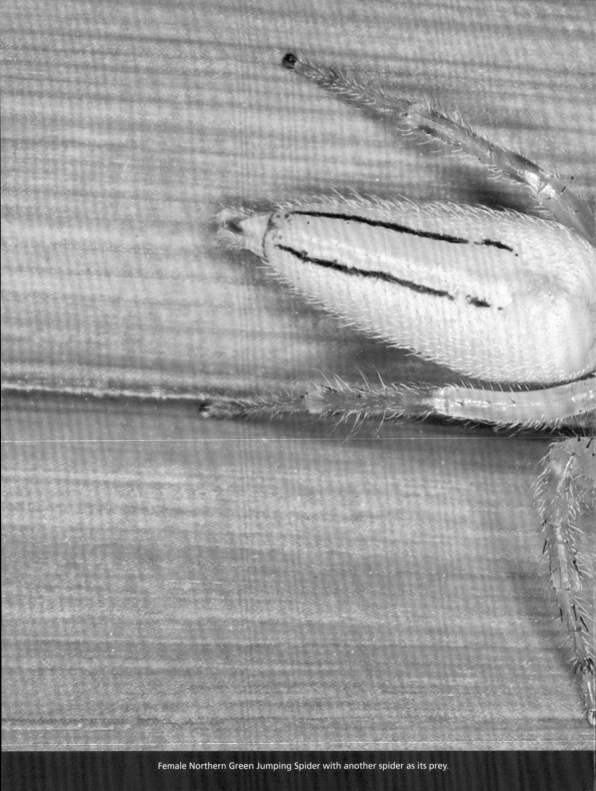

Female Northern Green Jumping Spider with another spider as its prey.

Lynx spider on a flower in the author's garden.

# LYNX SPIDER

*Oxyopes* species

Lynx spiders, which are found throughout eastern Australia, thrive in a wide range of habitats, including forests, woodlands and gardens, where they're discreetly camouflaged among flowers, grasses and the foliage of low shrubs.

They're highly distinctive spiders that measure a mere 1cm or less in length and that have an armoury of long and savage spines on their legs, and long, slender teardrop shaped abdomens with distinctive stripes in varying shades of brown.

Lynx spiders don't require a web or other trap in which to catch their prey, for with eight eyes and the ability to run and jump at great speed, these attractive little creatures are extremely efficient and ferocious hunters. They're on the prowl primarily during daylight hours, and hunt like the wild cats to which they owe their common name, for they slowly, stealthily and silently stalk their prey, then pounce with lightning speed. There's no escape for any minute creature that's destined to provide a meal for this prickly predator.

## WOLF SPIDER
Family Lycosidae

Early naturalists were convinced that spiders of the family Lycosidae hunted in packs, like wolves, and it was this assumption that gave them their common name. At most times of their lives, though, wolf spiders are solitary creatures.

More than 130 species of wolf spiders have been identified in Australia, but it's far

Wolf spider closing the lid of its burrow, near Taroom, Queensland.

from easy to distinguish one from another as many are of similar colour and there's considerable variation between the hues and patterns displayed by spiders of the same species. The majority, which are dull grey, brown or black, could never be described as glamorous, but all have one outstanding feature – their eyes.

Every wolf spider has eight eyes, including four small ones, one pair of large eyes that face forwards, and another pair of large eyes that face upwards, and this astounding optical array enables these ferocious predators to see in every direction simultaneously.

They thrive in a wide range of habitats, from rainforests, open grasslands and suburban gardens, to arid inland areas of the continent. While many live on the ground where they hunt among leaf litter and low vegetation for their prey, the species shown here has a very different lifestyle to that of its many relatives, for it spends much of its life in a burrow in the ground. It may occasionally emerge and hunt for prey, but it prefers the patient approach, and merely waits at the entrance to its burrow and snatches any insect that wanders within its reach, or takes pot luck and dines on any hapless creature that stumbles into its lair.

A wolf spider can sense the slightest of movements on the soil surrounding its burrow, and if a predator comes too close for comfort, this spider, which is often referred to as a 'trapdoor spider' – a name that is more commonly applied to members of various other spider families in the ancient infraorder Mygalomorphae – simply grabs the lid that it has created from grass and soil held together with silk, and pulls it down to seal itself inside its sanctuary until the danger has passed.

Female wolf spiders that live in burrows raise their young underground in silken webs, but other species, with dedication rivalling the maternal instinct of any human mother, never let their offspring out of their sight. Each carries her egg-sac with her, fixed to her spinnerets, and when the horde of tiny spiderlings hatch they instinctively clamber onto their mother's back and hold on tightly while she goes about her day-to-day life, but if she's threatened by another of her species, the spiderlings temporarily abandon her. She'll fight to the death to save herself and her young, but spiderlings have no parental loyalties, and when the battle comes to its conclusion, they scramble onto the back of the victor who carries them into their future.

Wolf spiders may demonstrate aggression towards each other, but although they pose no serious threat to humans, their bite can be extremely painful, with victims suffering from a range of unpleasant symptoms that ensure that their close encounters with these wild creatures are memorable ones for all the wrong reasons.

# INDEX

---

## OTHER TITLES BY THIS AUTHOR

*Encounters With Australian Birds*
ISBN 978 1 92554 695 8

*The Practical Gardener's Guide to Trees, Shrubs and Climbers*
ISBN 978 1 76079 442 2

For details of these books and hundreds of other Natural History titles see newhollandpublishers.com and follow ReedNewHolland on Facebook and Instagram